I am delighted to gift a free copy of my new cookbook

'The Fabulous Book of Dinners'

1st in my Follow-The-Flow Cookbooks series.

As you can see it is a beautifully stitched high quality hardback cookbook worth £25 of which I have put my heart and soul into and it would mean the world to me to help my cookbook series grow if you would share your amazing experience of cooking with my book on your social media or snap, tag & share on mine.

Thank you, your support is sincerely appreciated. Adrian

Follow-The-Flow Cookbooks

Follow our blog on Follow-the-flow.com

This is the first unedited edition

This book belongs to...

Date...

Hardback ISBN: 978-1-7394887-0-3
eBook ISBN: 978-1-7394887-1-0

INTRODUCTION

I have always had a passion for cooking and have usually been the family cook. Because much of the time we could not decide what to prepare for dinner, I would flick through the pages of a cookbook and ask my children to shout out "stop" and I would then cook that dish. Of course, this did not always work. Often, we would stop on starters, lunches or unsuitable dishes that the children did not want to eat. One dinnertime I was going through the cookbooks with my daughter, and said to her "if only we had a cookbook that was just dinners" and that's how the idea for this book came about.

In the process of thinking about a cookbook I hit upon an idea which seems to work very nicely. I selected our go-to family favourites and for the last few years I have been refining my recipes using my new approach to produce a cookbook that I hope is practical, easy to follow, and a joy to cook from.

Adrian Oades

This book is only to serve as a guide to cooking homemade food, as all kitchen equipment cookers, ovens, pots and pans vary in each household.

The notes page is to make any amendments to the recipe and to empower you to be creative.

A guide on how to use this book:

 # IMPORTANT

PREPARE YOUR INGREDIENTS FIRST

READ THE RECIPES FROM LEFT TO RIGHT

USE A TIMER

ALL THE RECIPES CAN BE CHANGED TO YOUR OWN TASTES.

HOPEFULLY YOU WILL CREATE YOUR OWN VARIATIONS.

The ingredients list is in order they appear in the main recipe and gives you the quantities you will need. The main recipe page tells you how to prepare and cook your food, and also allows you to familiarise yourself with the recipe.

The total time given for each recipe is approximate, as preparation is different for all of us.

There is an example on the next page of prepared food for your recipe. Rather than using lots of different bowls some prep can be immediately put into pans ready for cooking.

It is important to prepare all your ingredients first. In some instances (like roast dinner for example) your prep can take place whilst your chicken is cooking, this will save time.

Preparing your ingredients first eliminates the likelihood of burning food and allows you to cook in a calm and controlled manner.

Tablespoons and teaspoons are all level spoons.

Stock has been made using stock cubes.

Sugar unless otherwise stated is white granulated.

If your children are cooking dinner, never leave them unattended.

An example of a prepared food, before you start cooking
Spanish Omelette

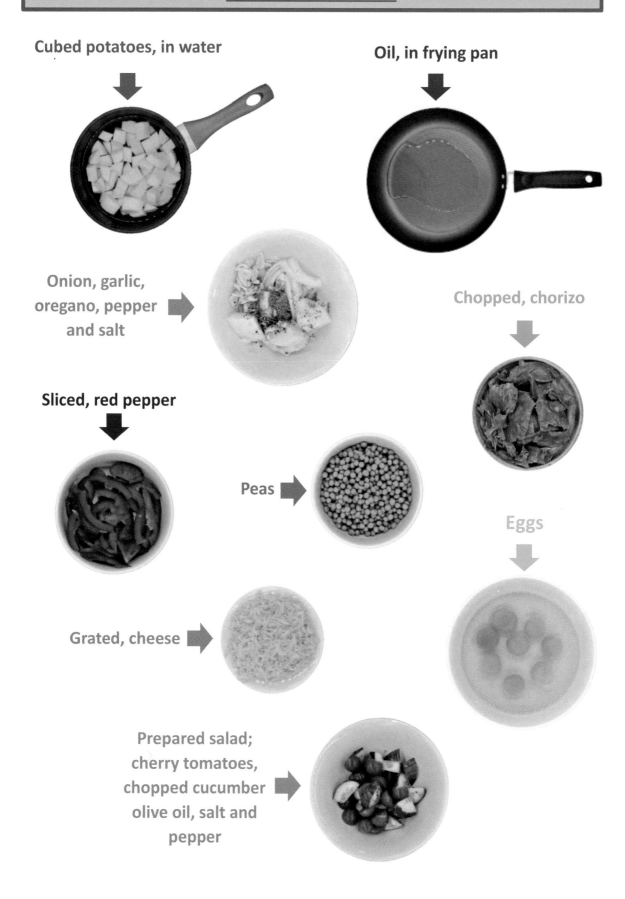

Cubed potatoes, in water

Oil, in frying pan

Onion, garlic, oregano, pepper and salt

Chopped, chorizo

Sliced, red pepper

Peas

Eggs

Grated, cheese

Prepared salad; cherry tomatoes, chopped cucumber olive oil, salt and pepper

Conversions, measurements and settings
All conversions are approximate

Grams	Millilitres	Tablespoons	Teaspoons	Cups	Ounces
15g	15ml	1 Tbs	3 tsp	1/16 cup	1/2 oz
30g	30ml	2 Tbs	6 tsp	1/8 cup	1 oz
60g	60ml	4 Tbs	12 tsp	1/4 cup	2 oz
85g	85ml	5 Tbs	16 tsp	1/3 cup	3 oz
115g	115ml	8 Tbs	24 tsp	1/2 cup	4 oz
140g	140ml	11 Tbs	32 tsp	2/3 cup	5 oz
180g	180ml	12 Tbs	36 tsp	3/4 cup	6 oz
225g	225ml	16 Tbs	48 tsp	1 cup	8 oz
450g	450ml	-	-	2 cups	16 oz
1000g	1000ml	-	-	4 1/4 cups	2.2lb

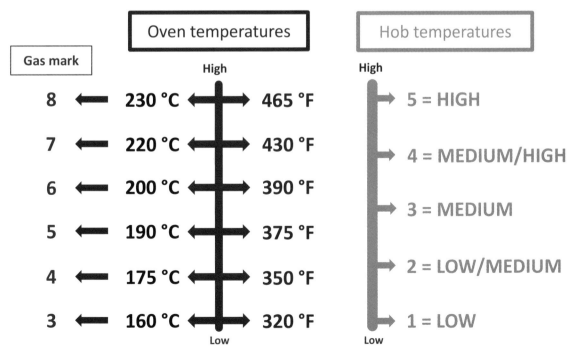

Gas mark	Oven temperatures		Hob temperatures
	High		High
8	230 °C	465 °F	5 = HIGH
7	220 °C	430 °F	4 = MEDIUM/HIGH
6	200 °C	390 °F	3 = MEDIUM
5	190 °C	375 °F	2 = LOW/MEDIUM
4	175 °C	350 °F	1 = LOW
3	160 °C	320 °F	
	Low		Low

INDEX

17. **Spanish Paella**

18. **King Prawn Linguine**

19. Cau Lau

20. Fajitas

21. **Lasagne**

22. **Salmon Ramen**

23. **Pizza**

24. **Beef Rendang**

25. **Burger and Chips**

26. **Roast Dinner**

27. **Creamy Vegetable Curry**

28. Macaroni Cheese

29. **Chicken and Rice**

30. **Shepherd's Pie**

31. Lamb Tagine

32. **Fish and Chips**

33. Roasted Red Pepper Pasta

34. **Chilli Con Carne**

Follow → The → Flow

AND ENJOY COOKING YOUR DINNER!

Thai Green Curry
Ingredients

325 grams Basmati Rice

650ml Cold Water

2 Small Shallots

1 or 2 Chilli Peppers

1 Stem Lemon Grass

2 Inch Piece Fresh Ginger

3 Cloves Garlic

20 grams Fresh Coriander

20 grams Fresh Thai Basil

Juice of ½ a Lime

1 Tablespoon of Vegetable Oil

2 Tablespoons of Water (if needed)

2 Tablespoons Vegetable Oil

400ml Coconut Milk

300ml Chicken Stock

650 grams Cubed Chicken

½ Medium Aubergine

1 Teaspoon Salt

½ Teaspoon Black Pepper

1 Teaspoon Palm Sugar

1 Teaspoon Fish Sauce

250 grams Raw Prawns

100 grams Mushrooms

2 Medium Tomatoes

1 Sliced Green Pepper

4 Sliced Spring Onions

Juice ½ Lime

5 grams Fresh Thai Basil

NOTES;

Long grain rice can be used, rinse the rice then place in plenty of cold water, bring to the boil, simmer for 10/12 minutes, drain and serve.

Blending the paste ingredients is the quickest and best way.

Palm sugar is best, any type is ok.

Use a good quality coconut milk.

For vegan option replace the meats with butternut squash and the stock with vegetable.

1

Thai Green Curry

Authentic Thai curry that you will cook again and again.

Serves 5

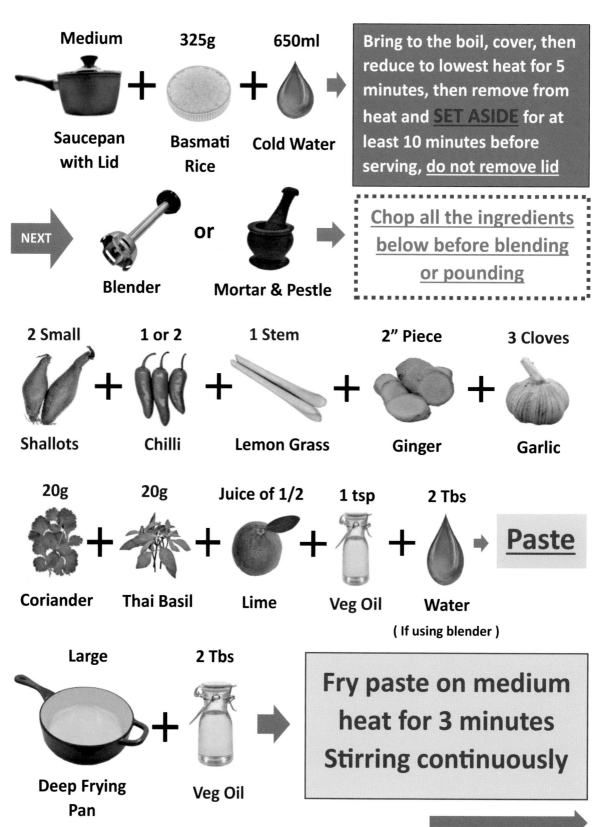

Medium — Saucepan with Lid
+
325g — Basmati Rice
+
650ml — Cold Water
→
Bring to the boil, cover, then reduce to lowest heat for 5 minutes, then remove from heat and SET ASIDE for at least 10 minutes before serving, do not remove lid

NEXT →
Blender **or** Mortar & Pestle →
Chop all the ingredients below before blending or pounding

2 Small — Shallots
+
1 or 2 — Chilli
+
1 Stem — Lemon Grass
+
2" Piece — Ginger
+
3 Cloves — Garlic

20g — Coriander
+
20g — Thai Basil
+
Juice of 1/2 — Lime
+
1 tsp — Veg Oil
+
2 Tbs — Water
→
Paste

(If using blender)

Large — Deep Frying Pan
+
2 Tbs — Veg Oil
→
Fry paste on medium heat for 3 minutes Stirring continuously

1

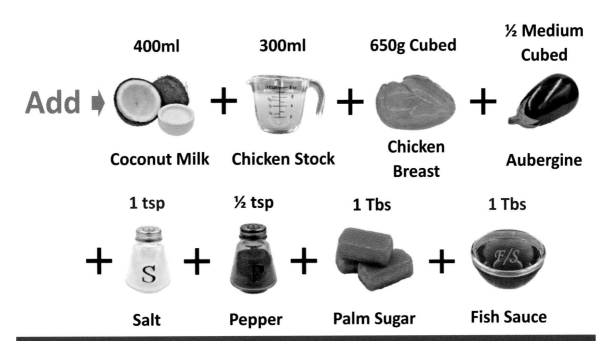

Add ➡

400ml	300ml	650g Cubed	½ Medium Cubed
Coconut Milk	Chicken Stock	Chicken Breast	Aubergine

1 tsp	½ tsp	1 Tbs	1 Tbs
Salt	Pepper	Palm Sugar	Fish Sauce

Cook for 15 minutes on a med/high heat, stir occasionally

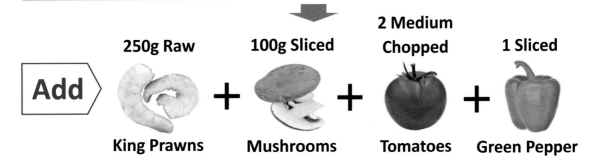

Add

250g Raw	100g Sliced	2 Medium Chopped	1 Sliced
King Prawns	Mushrooms	Tomatoes	Green Pepper

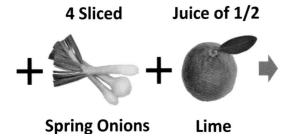

4 Sliced	Juice of 1/2
Spring Onions	Lime

Cook for 5 minutes on medium heat, remove from heat and serve with the rice

Sprinkle over some chopped Thai Basil ➡

YOUR NOTES

Tomato and Orange Spaghetti
Ingredients

2 Tablespoons Olive Oil

1 Grated Carrot

1 Onion

3 Cloves Garlic

5 Large Tomatoes

1 Tablespoon Tomato Puree

1 Tablespoon Dried Oregano

1 Teaspoon Salt

½ Teaspoon Black Pepper

250ml Water

Juice of 1 Orange

Small Handful Fresh Basil (20 grams)

Water for Pasta

400 grams Dried Spaghetti

NOTES;

Add extra water to sauce if required.

If blending allow sauce to cool.

Any pasta can be used.

2

Tomato and Orange Spaghetti

Really tasty simple pasta sauce with a sweet kick from the orange. Tinned tomatoes can be used.

Serves 4

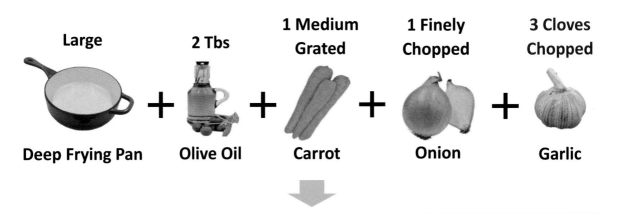

Large	2 Tbs	1 Medium Grated	1 Finely Chopped	3 Cloves Chopped
Deep Frying Pan	Olive Oil	Carrot	Onion	Garlic

Fry for 5 minutes on Med/High heat stirring regularly

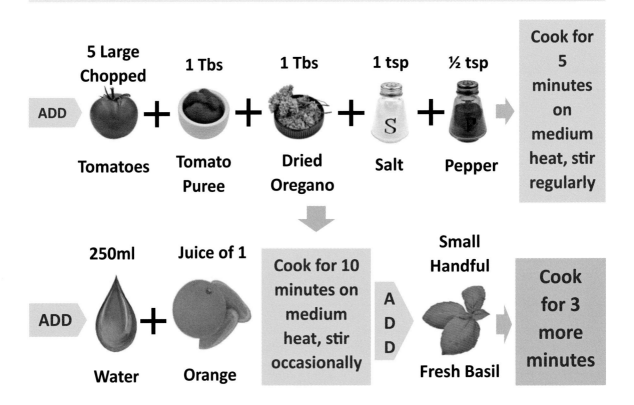

ADD

5 Large Chopped	1 Tbs	1 Tbs	1 tsp	½ tsp	Cook for 5 minutes on medium heat, stir regularly
Tomatoes	Tomato Puree	Dried Oregano	Salt	Pepper	

ADD

250ml	Juice of 1	Cook for 10 minutes on medium heat, stir occasionally	ADD	Small Handful	Cook for 3 more minutes
Water	Orange			Fresh Basil	

Whilst cooking the sauce, start pasta

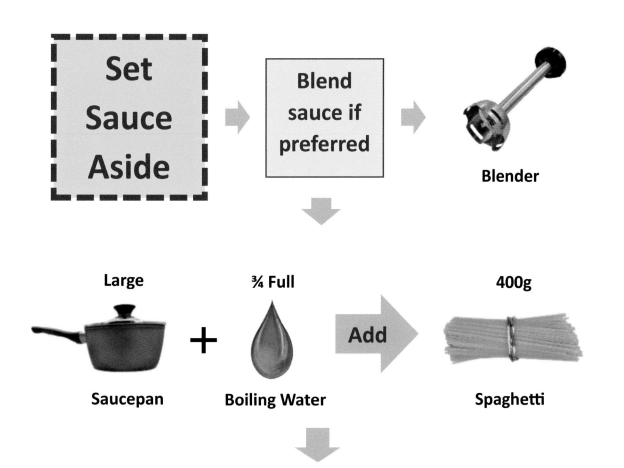

Set Sauce Aside → **Blend sauce if preferred** → **Blender**

Large Saucepan + **¾ Full** Boiling Water **Add** → **400g** Spaghetti

Cook on a medium heat for 9 minutes

Drain Spaghetti → Mix with Sauce

Serve with grated cheese of your choice → **Grated** Cheese →

YOUR NOTES

Mince in the Oven
Ingredients

Water for Carrots

6 Large Carrots

1 Teaspoon Sugar

1 Teaspoon Salt

2 Tablespoons Vegetable Oil

3 Large Onions

1 Teaspoon Black Pepper

750 grams Minced Beef

300ml Beef Stock

Water to Cover Meat

Water for Potatoes

1.2 Kilos Potatoes

2 Tins Baked Beans (800 grams)

NOTES;

Make sure the mixture doesn't dry out whilst in the oven; by the end of cooking the water you put in should be reduced and you should have a nice thick sauce.

Mash the potatoes if you prefer, even serve with chips.

Use plant-based mince and vegetable stock as a vegan alternative, and add a teaspoon of yeast extract.

Mince in the Oven

Use large oven tray and set oven temperature at 220°c.

My kids love this dish. Serves 6

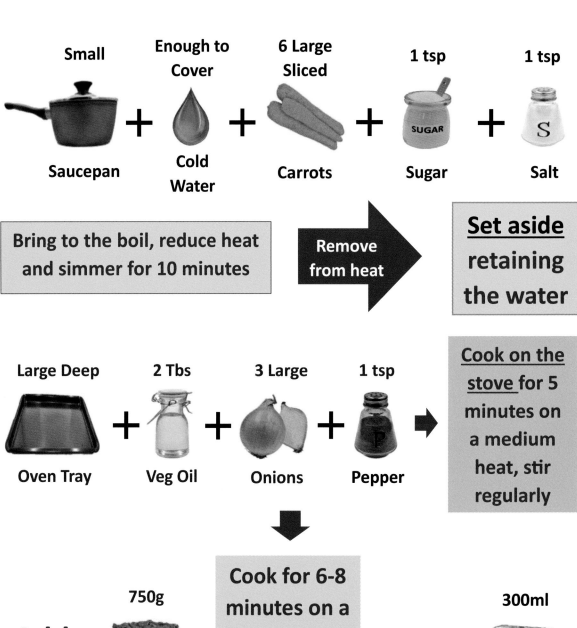

Small + **Cold Water** (Enough to Cover) + **Carrots** (6 Large Sliced) + **Sugar** (1 tsp) + **Salt** (1 tsp)

Saucepan

Bring to the boil, reduce heat and simmer for 10 minutes

Remove from heat

Set aside retaining the water

Large Deep (Oven Tray) + **Veg Oil** (2 Tbs) + **Onions** (3 Large) + **Pepper** (1 tsp)

Cook on the stove for 5 minutes on a medium heat, stir regularly

Add to the onions → **Minced Beef** (750g) → Cook for 6-8 minutes on a high/med heat until the meat is well-browned → **Add** → **Beef Stock** (300ml)

Add ➤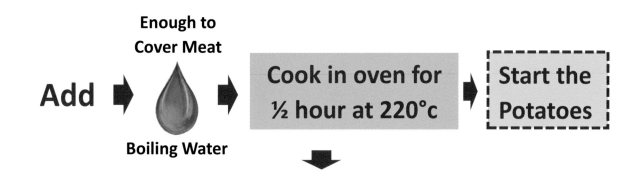

Enough to Cover Meat

Boiling Water

➤ **Cook in oven for ½ hour at 220°c** ➤ **Start the Potatoes**

⬇

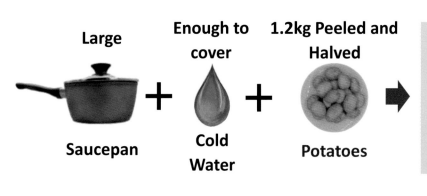

Large

Saucepan

➕

Enough to cover

Cold Water

➕

1.2kg Peeled and Halved

Potatoes

➤ **Bring to boil then simmer for 20 minutes, drain, the potatoes are ready to serve**

Add

To the meat and onions

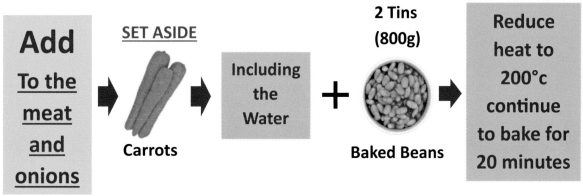

SET ASIDE

Carrots

➤ **Including the Water** ➕

2 Tins (800g)

Baked Beans

➤ **Reduce heat to 200°c continue to bake for 20 minutes**

⬇

Remove from the oven, serve the meat and potatoes together ➤

Cumin Dal and Garlic Dal
Ingredients

Cumin Dal/Garlic Dal

300 grams Red Lentils

1 ½ Teaspoons Salt

Rice

300 grams Basmati Rice

600ml Cold Water

Cumin Dal

2 Tablespoons Vegetable Oil

2 Tablespoons Yellow Mustard Seeds

2 Tablespoons Cumin Seeds

1 Small Onion

2 Cloves Garlic

2 Sliced Green Chillies

1 Teaspoon Ground Cumin

1 Teaspoon Ground Turmeric

2 Tomatoes

20 grams Fresh Coriander

Garlic Dal

4 Tablespoons Vegetable Oil

3 Whole Cloves

2 Whole Fresh Chillies

8 Large Cloves Garlic

1 Teaspoon Asafoetida

NOTES;

The mixture that is made before adding lentils is called the Masala, you can experiment with this and make endless variations.

Ladle the lentils into the hot Masala, make sure the Masala is off the heat.

Flat bread is traditionally eaten with Dal.

4

Cumin Dal and Garlic Dal

Two different Dals to try. Serve with flat breads or rice. Made the same way so 300 grams of lentils is enough for both dishes.

Serves 6

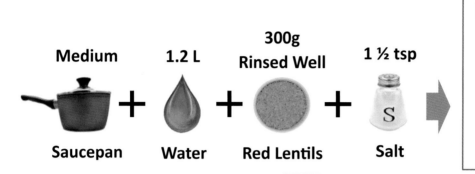

Medium | 1.2 L | 300g Rinsed Well | 1 ½ tsp

Saucepan + Water + Red Lentils + Salt

Bring to boil, remove the scum and simmer for 15 minutes **SET ASIDE**

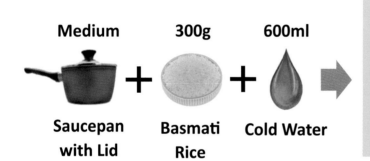

Medium | 300g | 600ml

Saucepan with Lid + Basmati Rice + Cold Water

Bring to the boil, cover, then reduce to lowest heat for 5 minutes remove from heat and **SET ASIDE** for at least 10 minutes until serving, do not remove lid

Cumin Dal

Small | 2 Tbs | 2 tsp | 2 tsp

Saucepan + Veg Oil + Yellow Mustard Seeds + Cumin Seeds

Fry for 1 minute on med/high heat or until seeds start to pop

Add

1 Small Chopped | 2 Cloves Chopped | 2 Sliced

Onion + Garlic + Green Chillies

Fry for 3-4 minutes on medium heat until golden, stir regularly

4

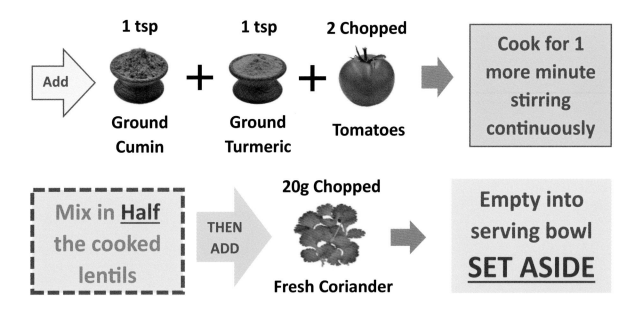

Add → **1 tsp** Ground Cumin **+** **1 tsp** Ground Turmeric **+** **2 Chopped** Tomatoes → Cook for 1 more minute stirring continuously

Mix in **Half** the cooked lentils → **THEN ADD** → **20g Chopped** Fresh Coriander → Empty into serving bowl **SET ASIDE**

Garlic Dal

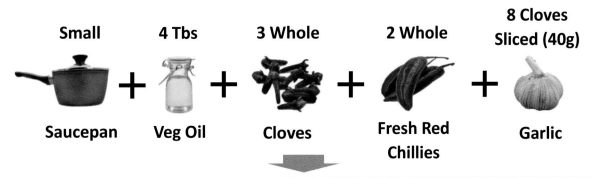

Small Saucepan **+** **4 Tbs** Veg Oil **+** **3 Whole** Cloves **+** **2 Whole** Fresh Red Chillies **+** **8 Cloves Sliced (40g)** Garlic

Fry on low/medium heat for 2 minutes until garlic is golden brown, stirring continually

Then add → **1 tsp** Asafoetida → Cook for 1 more minute, stir continuously → Mix with remaining cooked lentils and serve with the Cumin Dal and rice

Cumin

Garlic

Mushroom Risotto

Ingredients

2 Tablespoons Olive Oil

50 grams Butter

1 Large Onion

3 Cloves Garlic

250 grams Chestnut Mushrooms

200 grams Arborio Rice

100ml White Wine

300ml Chicken or Vegetable Stock

1 Teaspoon Salt

½ Teaspoon Black Pepper

200ml Water

Juice of ½ Lemon

20 grams Parsley

Knob of Butter

½ Cucumber

1 Little Gem Lettuce

Juice of ½ Lemon

NOTES;

Small cubes of sweet potato, courgette or aubergine can replace the mushrooms.

You can use any vegetable you desire.

For vegan option replace butter with a dairy free alternative and the chicken stock with vegetable stock.

Mushroom Risotto

The variations with risotto are endless, you basically coat the rice in some form of oil, then add double the volume of liquid to rice and cook for approximately 20 minutes.

Serves 4

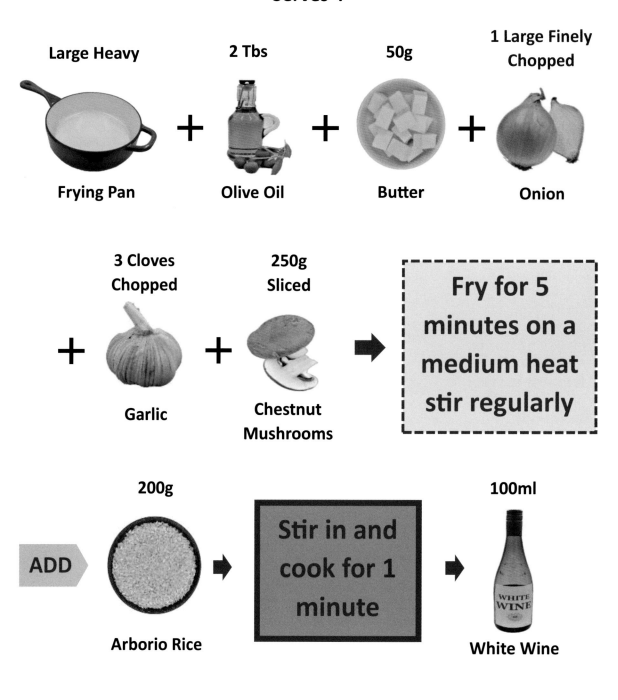

Large Heavy
Frying Pan

2 Tbs
Olive Oil

50g
Butter

1 Large Finely Chopped
Onion

3 Cloves Chopped
Garlic

250g Sliced
Chestnut Mushrooms

Fry for 5 minutes on a medium heat stir regularly

200g
Arborio Rice

ADD

Stir in and cook for 1 minute

100ml
White Wine

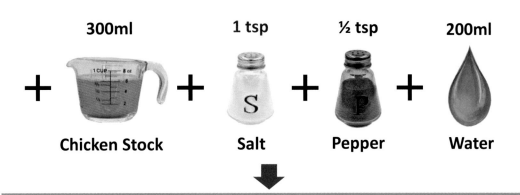

	300ml		1 tsp		½ tsp		200ml
+	Chicken Stock	+	Salt	+	Pepper	+	Water

cook for 20 minutes on a medium heat stir occasionally

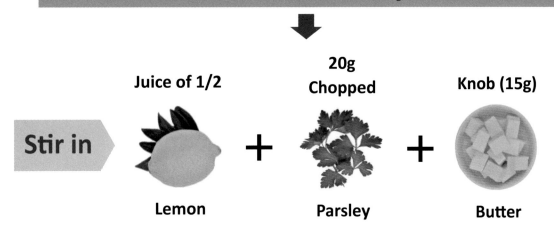

Stir in | Juice of 1/2 Lemon | + | 20g Chopped Parsley | + | Knob (15g) Butter

Serve with salad

½ in Small Cubes

Cucumber

1 Sliced

Little Gem Lettuce

Juice of ½

Lemon

Malaysian Chicken Curry
Ingredients

3 Tablespoons Vegetable Oil

4 Whole Cardamom Pods

6 Whole Cloves

2 Sticks Cinnamon

2 Whole Star Anise

1 Large Onion

3 Cloves Garlic

1-2 Chillies

2 Inch Piece Fresh Ginger

1 Stem Lemon Grass

8 Fresh Curry Leaves

2 Tablespoons Mild Curry Powder

2 Tablespoons Water

400ml Coconut Milk

300ml Chicken Stock

2 Tablespoons Tamarind Water

750 grams Cubed Chicken

2 Medium Potatoes

1 Teaspoon Salt

½ Teaspoon Black Pepper

2 Teaspoons Palm Sugar

1 Teaspoon Ground Turmeric

350 grams Basmati Rice

Water for Rice (700ml)

2 Large Tomatoes

NOTES;

I use wet Tamarind; it's sold in a block. Break off a piece about the volume of two stock cubes, soak in hot water (75ml) for 5 minutes use a spoon to break it up then strain off the fibre (retaining the water), alternatively buy a tamarind paste and only use 1 teaspoon.

Cut the potatoes approximately the size of half a golf ball.

Remove whole spices at the end if you prefer.

For vegan option replace chicken stock with vegetable and meat with cubed butternut squash and cubed sweet potato.

Malaysian Chicken Curry

This is a mild-sweet curry from Borneo.   Serves 6

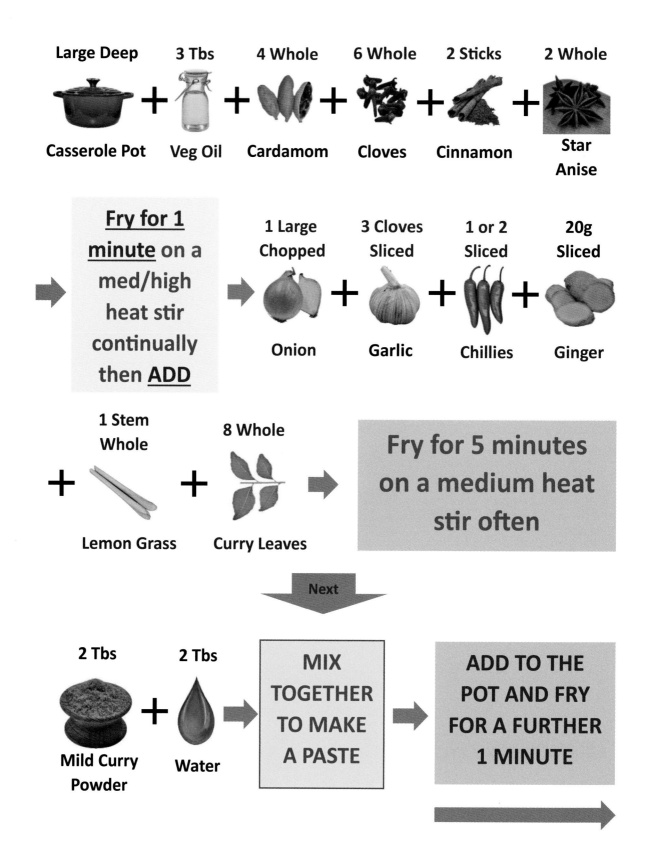

Large Deep	3 Tbs	4 Whole	6 Whole	2 Sticks	2 Whole
Casserole Pot	Veg Oil	Cardamom	Cloves	Cinnamon	Star Anise

Fry for 1 minute on a med/high heat stir continually then **ADD**

1 Large Chopped	3 Cloves Sliced	1 or 2 Sliced	20g Sliced
Onion	Garlic	Chillies	Ginger

1 Stem Whole — Lemon Grass

8 Whole — Curry Leaves

Fry for 5 minutes on a medium heat stir often

Next

2 Tbs	2 Tbs
Mild Curry Powder	Water

MIX TOGETHER TO MAKE A PASTE

ADD TO THE POT AND FRY FOR A FURTHER 1 MINUTE

Add

400ml	300ml	75ml	750g Cubed
Coconut Milk	Chicken Stock	Tamarind Water (See Notes)	Chicken Breast

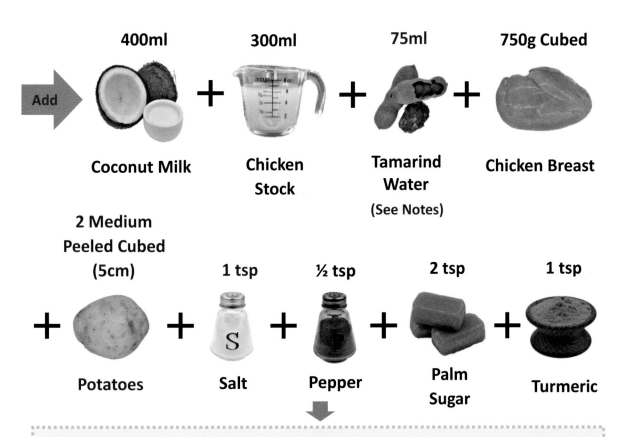

2 Medium Peeled Cubed (5cm)	1 tsp	½ tsp	2 tsp	1 tsp
Potatoes	Salt	Pepper	Palm Sugar	Turmeric

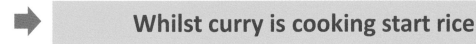

Cook for 20 minutes on a high/med heat stir occasionally

Whilst curry is cooking start rice

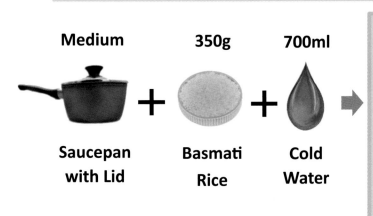

Medium	350g	700ml
Saucepan with Lid	Basmati Rice	Cold Water

Bring to the boil, cover, then reduce to lowest heat for 5 minutes then remove from heat and set aside for at least 10 minutes until serving, do not remove lid

ADD TO CURRY

2 Chopped

Tomatoes

Cook for 3 minutes and serve with rice

Vegetable Risotto

Ingredients

3 Tablespoons Olive Oil

1 Large Onion

3 Cloves Garlic

1 Medium Courgette

1 Teaspoon Salt

½ Teaspoon Black Pepper

½ Red Pepper

½ Green Pepper

150 grams French Beans

1 Stick Celery

½ Teaspoon Sweet Paprika

350 grams Arborio Rice

100ml White Wine

700ml Chicken or Vegetable Stock

400 grams (1 can) Chickpeas

15 grams Parsley

2 Large Tomatoes

Juice of ½ a Lemon

NOTES;

Try using different vegetables or whatever needs using up.

Leave out the wine for a slightly different flavour.

For a meat option, add cubed chicken when frying the onions.

Vegetable Risotto

Any type of vegetable can be used with this delicious Risotto, change the chickpeas for butterbeans if you like. Serves 6

Large Deep — Frying Pan with Lid

+ 3 Tbs — Olive Oil

+ 1 Large Chopped — Onion

+ 3 Cloves Chopped — Garlic

+ 1 Medium Cubed — Courgette

Cook on med/low heat for 4 minutes stir regularly THEN ADD

1 tsp — Salt

+ ½ tsp — Black Pepper

+ ½ Sliced — Red Pepper

+ ½ Sliced — Green Pepper

+ 150g Whole — French Bean

+ 1 Stick Finely Chopped — Celery

+ ½ tsp — Sweet Paprika

Cook on med/low heat for 3 minutes stir regularly

THEN ADD — 350g — Arborio Rice

Coat the rice well

THEN ADD — 100ml — White Wine

+ 700ml — Veg Stock

+ 1 Tin (400g) — Chickpeas

Bring to boil, <u>cover</u> then reduce to lowest heat, cook for 15 minutes until most of the water has been absorbed, stir occasionally.

Turn off heat then <u>MIX IN</u> and <u>SERVE</u>

15g Chopped

Parsley

2 Large Chopped

Tomatoes

Juice of ½

Lemon

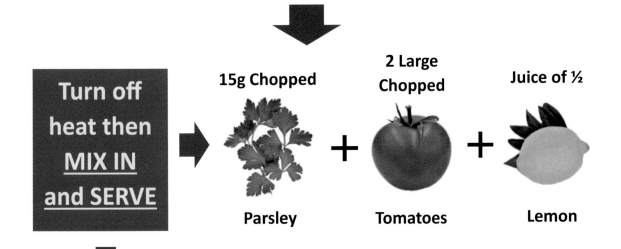

YOUR NOTES

Spaghetti Bolognese

Ingredients

3 Tablespoons Olive Oil

2 Medium Onions

4 Cloves Garlic

1 Tablespoon Dried Oregano

½ Teaspoon Black Pepper

1 Tablespoon Tomato Puree

500 grams Minced Beef

6 Large Tomatoes

400ml Beef Stock

Juice of ½ a Lemon

½ Teaspoon Salt

Water for Pasta

450g Spaghetti

NOTES;

Add grated carrot and finely chopped celery at the start (with the onions) for a different take on this dish.

You can also include sliced mushrooms and sliced red pepper.

Add more water for a wetter sauce.

For vegan option replace meat with plant-based mince and stock with vegetable stock.

Spaghetti Bolognese

A family favourite.   Serves 5

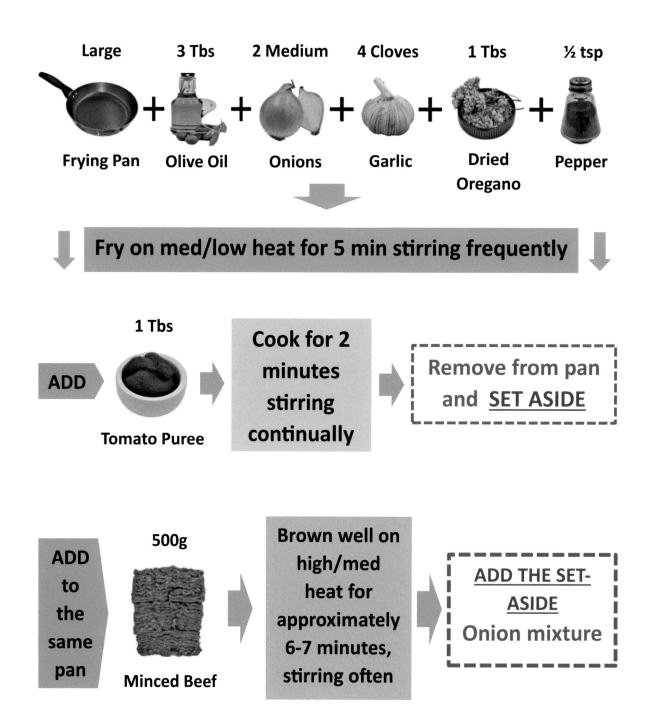

Large	3 Tbs	2 Medium	4 Cloves	1 Tbs	½ tsp
Frying Pan	Olive Oil	Onions	Garlic	Dried Oregano	Pepper

Fry on med/low heat for 5 min stirring frequently

ADD 1 Tbs Tomato Puree → **Cook for 2 minutes stirring continually** → Remove from pan and **SET ASIDE**

ADD to the same pan 500g Minced Beef → **Brown well on high/med heat for approximately 6-7 minutes, stirring often** → **ADD THE SET-ASIDE** Onion mixture

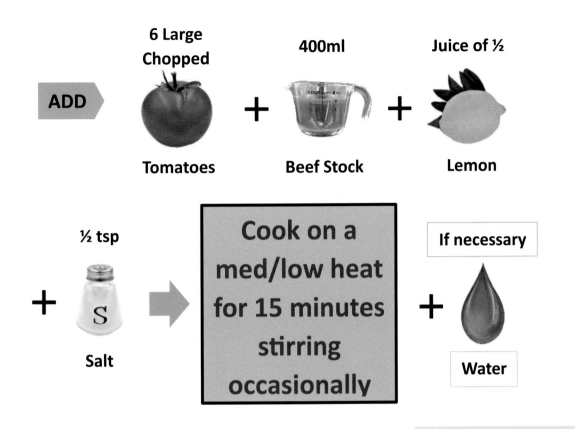

ADD

6 Large Chopped — Tomatoes + **400ml** — Beef Stock + **Juice of ½** — Lemon

+ **½ tsp** — Salt → **Cook on a med/low heat for 15 minutes stirring occasionally** + **If necessary** — Water

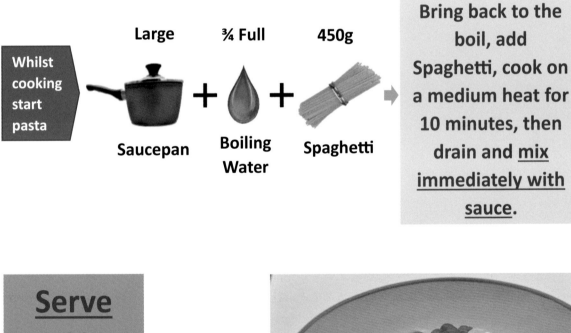

Whilst cooking start pasta — **Large** — Saucepan + **¾ Full** — Boiling Water + **450g** — Spaghetti → **Bring back to the boil, add Spaghetti, cook on a medium heat for 10 minutes, then drain and mix immediately with sauce.**

Serve Add a grated cheese of your choice → **Grated** — Cheese →

Kedgeree

Ingredients

Water for Eggs

6 Large Eggs

800ml Water

Water for Poaching Fish

450 grams Smoked Haddock

2 Bay Leaves

3 Tablespoons Vegetable Oil

1 Large Onion

2 Cloves Garlic

½ Teaspoon Black Pepper

½ Teaspoon Ground Turmeric

1 Tablespoon Curry Powder

2 Teaspoons Water

350 grams Basmati Rice

150 grams Peas

½ Teaspoon Salt

150ml Vegetable Stock

20 grams Fresh Parsley

Juice of ½ Lemon

NOTES;

Any curry power can be used, I use a mild one.

Flake the fish when cooled.

For vegan option replace the fish with a root vegetable and omit the eggs.

Kedgeree

A great filling dish that's quick and easy.   Serves 6

Medium + **Enough to Cover** + **6 Large**

Saucepan   Cold Water   Eggs

Bring eggs to the boil then simmer for 8 minutes, remove from heat, run cold water into the saucepan when cool enough to handle, peel the eggs then **SET ASIDE**

Large + **800ml** + **450g** + **2 Whole**

Saucepan   Cold Water   Smoked Haddock   Bay leaves

Poach; Bring to boiling point then turn off heat, after 5 minutes drain and RETAIN THE WATER remove bay leaves and peppercorns and **SET ASIDE**

Large deep + **3 Tbs** + **1 Large** + **2 Cloves** + **½ tsp**

Frying Pan with Lid   Veg Oil   Onion   Garlic   Black Pepper

Fry for 5 minutes on med/low heat stirring often

Mix together to make a paste

Small + **½ tsp** + **1 Tbs** + **2 tsp**

Bowl   Ground Turmeric   Curry Powder   Water

Add paste to onion mixture, stir continually

THEN ADD

350g **Basmati Rice** + 150g **Peas** + ½ tsp **Salt** → **Cook for 1 minute coating all the rice**

ADD ~~RETAINED WATER~~ (600ml) + 150ml **Vegetable Stock** → **Bring to boiling point reduce heat to low heat, cover and cook for 15 minutes, stir occasionally**

Turn off heat, leave to stand- covered for 5 minutes → **Meanwhile flake the cooled fish removing the skin**

Mix into the rice mixture → Flaked **Smoked Haddock** + 20g Chopped **Fresh Parsley** + Juice of ½ **Lemon** + Quartered **Hard Boiled Eggs**

SERVE →

9

YOUR NOTES

Fish Pie

Ingredients

Water for Potatoes

1.5 kilos Potatoes

Knob of Butter

1 Tablespoon Milk

½ Teaspoon Salt

400ml Milk

750 grams Fish Pie Mix (Haddock, Cod and Salmon)

1 Medium Onion

2 Bay Leaves

5 Whole Cloves

8 Whole Peppercorns

250 grams Raw King Prawns

3 Tablespoons Vegetable Oil

4 Tablespoons Plain Flour

1 Teaspoon Dijon Mustard

¼ Teaspoon Grated Nutmeg

1 Teaspoon Salt

½ Teaspoon Black Pepper

30 grams Parsley

Water for Peas

350 grams Peas

NOTES;

Soya milk is a good dairy free alternative to dairy milk; however, any other plant-based milk can be used.

Allow mixture to cool before topping with mash potato.

A vegan alternative could be cubed potatoes, cubed sweet potato, butternut squash or butter beans.

You can also top with cheese or two slices of toast chopped up finely and soaked in olive oil.

Any type of prawn can be used.

Fish Pie

A creamy fish pie that can be made with either dairy milk or a dairy free alternative, with or without prawns. Set oven temperature to 220°c   Serves 6

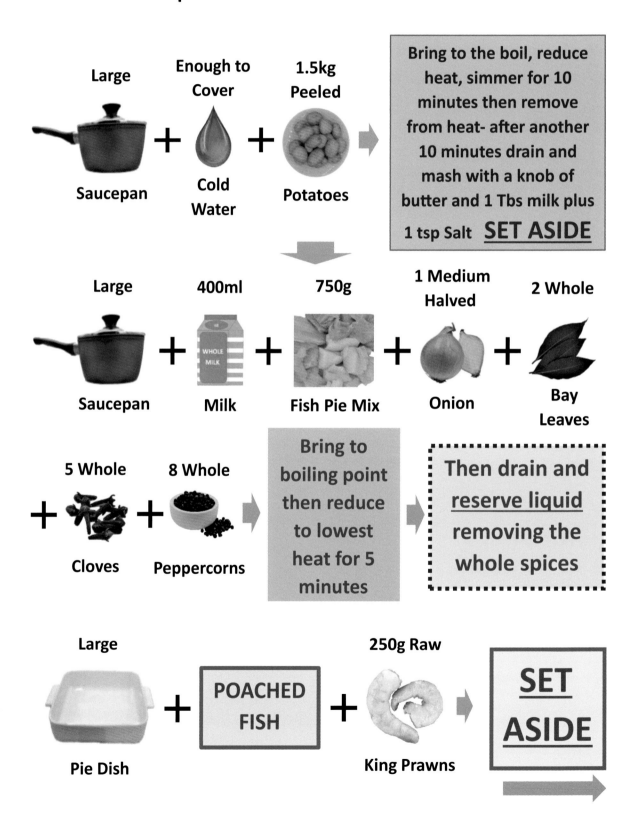

Large Saucepan + **Enough to Cover** Cold Water + **1.5kg Peeled** Potatoes →

Bring to the boil, reduce heat, simmer for 10 minutes then remove from heat- after another 10 minutes drain and mash with a knob of butter and 1 Tbs milk plus 1 tsp Salt **SET ASIDE**

Large Saucepan + **400ml** Milk + **750g** Fish Pie Mix + **1 Medium Halved** Onion + **2 Whole** Bay Leaves

+ **5 Whole** Cloves + **8 Whole** Peppercorns →

Bring to boiling point then reduce to lowest heat for 5 minutes →

Then drain and reserve liquid removing the whole spices

Large Pie Dish + POACHED FISH + **250g Raw** King Prawns → SET ASIDE

| **Make A Rue** → | **Medium**
 Saucepan | + | **3 Tbs**
 Veg Oil | + | **4 Tbs**
 FLOUR
 Plain Flour | → | Cook for 3 minutes on a medium heat stirring continuously |

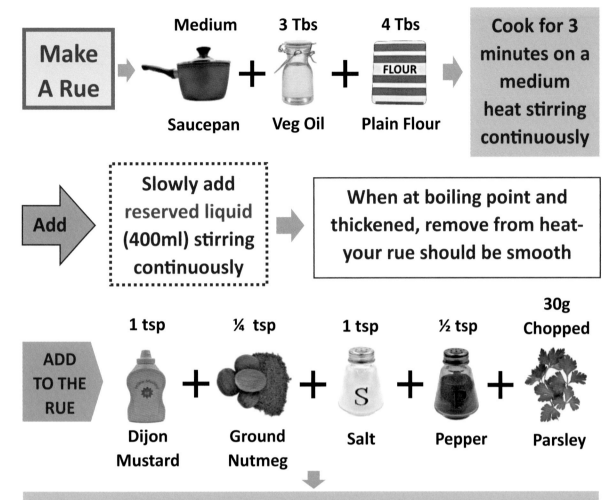

Add → Slowly add reserved liquid (400ml) stirring continuously → When at boiling point and thickened, remove from heat- your rue should be smooth

ADD TO THE RUE →

| **1 tsp**
 Dijon Mustard | + | **¼ tsp**
 Ground Nutmeg | + | **1 tsp**
 Salt | + | **½ tsp**
 Pepper | + | **30g** Chopped
 Parsley |

Mix the sauce with the SET-ASIDE fish, top evenly with the SET-ASIDE mash potato, rough up the mash potato with a fork and bake for 20 minutes at 220°c

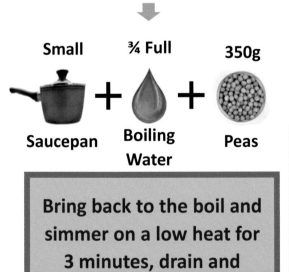

| **Small**
 Saucepan | + | **¾ Full**
 Boiling Water | + | **350g**
 Peas |

Bring back to the boil and simmer on a low heat for 3 minutes, drain and serve with the fish pie →

Creamy Mushroom Pasta

Ingredients

2 Tablespoons Olive Oil

Knob of Butter

1 Medium Onion

3 Cloves Garlic

500 grams Chestnut Mushrooms

¼ Teaspoon Black Pepper

250ml Chicken Stock

1 Tablespoon Cornflour

3 Tablespoons Water

100 grams Grated Cheddar Cheese

200ml Double Cream

¼ Teaspoon Salt

¼ Teaspoon Black Pepper

350 grams Pasta

Water for Pasta

NOTES;

Medium cheddar cheese works for me, you choose.

Make sure not to burn the onions and mushrooms however they need to be well-browned.

It doesn't really matter what mushrooms you use; chestnut mushrooms work for me.

Use any type of pasta.

For dairy free: replace cream with soya milk add an extra teaspoon of corn flour, use a dairy free butter.

Creamy Mushroom Pasta

Really delicious, very quick, very easy, very Mushroom!

Serves 4

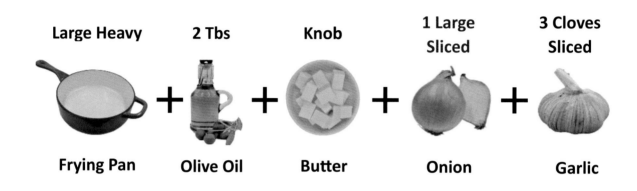

Large Heavy + **2 Tbs** + **Knob** + **1 Large Sliced** + **3 Cloves Sliced**

Frying Pan   **Olive Oil**   **Butter**   **Onion**   **Garlic**

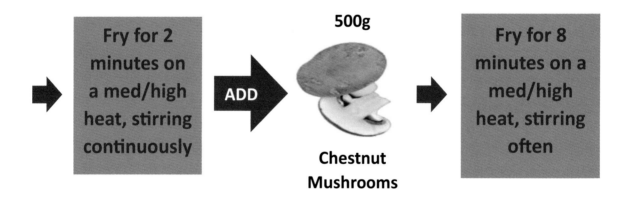

Fry for 2 minutes on a med/high heat, stirring continuously

ADD

500g

Chestnut Mushrooms

Fry for 8 minutes on a med/high heat, stirring often

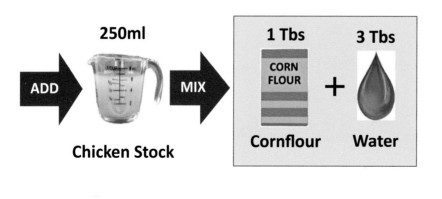

ADD

250ml

Chicken Stock

MIX

1 Tbs CORN FLOUR + **3 Tbs**

Cornflour   Water

Add to pan stirring continuously

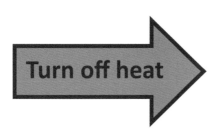

Turn off heat → Allow to cool for 2 minutes

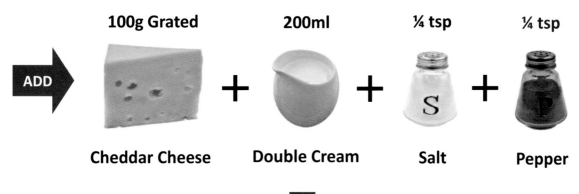

100g Grated	200ml	¼ tsp	¼ tsp

ADD

Cheddar Cheese + Double Cream + Salt + Pepper

SET ASIDE SAUCE → RE-HEAT JUST BEFORE ADDING TO THE PASTA

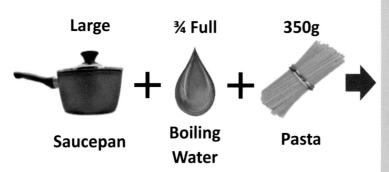

Large + ¾ Full + 350g

Saucepan + Boiling Water + Pasta →

Add pasta to boiling water, bring back to boiling point simmer on medium heat for 10 minutes, then drain

Add pasta to the mushroom sauce →

Sausage, Mash and Onion Gravy

Ingredients

1 Teaspoon Olive Oil

8 Sausages

1.2kg Potatoes

Water for Potatoes

1 Teaspoon Salt

Knob of Butter

3 Tablespoons Milk

1 Raw Egg

¼ Teaspoon Black Pepper

2 Tablespoons Olive Oil

1 Large Onion

2 Cloves Garlic

¼ Teaspoon Black Pepper

1 Tablespoon Corn Flour

400ml Beef Stock

¼ Teaspoon Salt

Water for Peas

400 grams Peas

NOTES;

Buy a good quality sausage.

For a dairy-free option use dairy free butter and soya milk leave out the egg, replace the stock with vegetable stock. Use vegan Sausages.

For a thicker gravy add ½ a tablespoon of corn flour .

Plain flour can replace corn flour.

Sausage, Mash and Onion Gravy

Always a good choice, I love it and so do the kids...
Set oven temperature at 200°c.   Serves 4

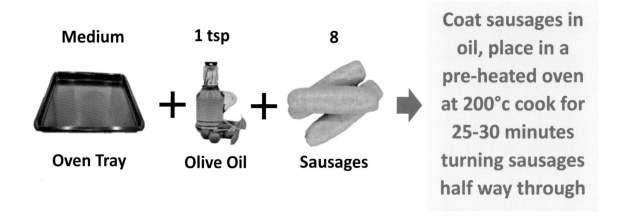

Medium	1 tsp	8	Coat sausages in oil, place in a pre-heated oven at 200°c cook for 25-30 minutes turning sausages half way through
Oven Tray	Olive Oil	Sausages	

 Whilst the sausages are cooking

Large	1.2kg Peeled	Enough to Cover	1 tsp	Bring to boil then simmer for 20 minutes drain
Saucepan	Potatoes	Water	Salt	

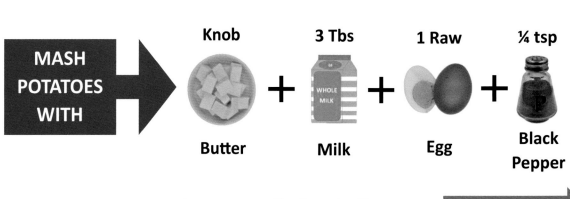

MASH POTATOES WITH

Knob	3 Tbs	1 Raw	¼ tsp
Butter	Milk	Egg	Black Pepper

Whilst the sausages and potatoes are cooking

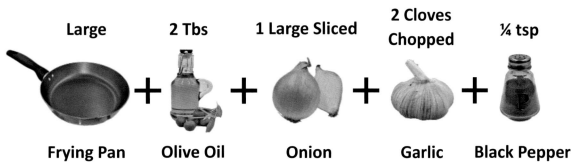

Large	2 Tbs	1 Large Sliced	2 Cloves Chopped	¼ tsp
Frying Pan	Olive Oil	Onion	Garlic	Black Pepper

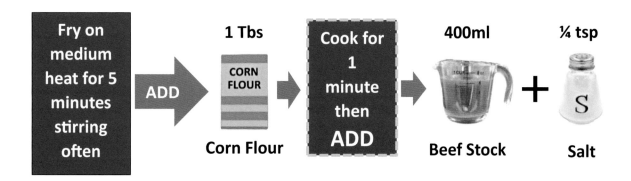

Fry on medium heat for 5 minutes stirring often

ADD

1 Tbs — Corn Flour

Cook for 1 minute then ADD

400ml — Beef Stock

¼ tsp — Salt

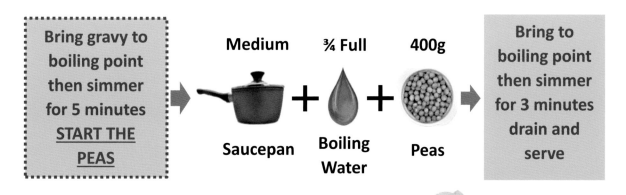

Bring gravy to boiling point then simmer for 5 minutes **START THE PEAS**

Medium — Saucepan

¾ Full — Boiling Water

400g — Peas

Bring to boiling point then simmer for 3 minutes drain and serve

Bring the sausages, mash and peas together and serve with the gravy

12

YOUR NOTES

Meatballs with Tagliatelle and Garlic Bread

Ingredients

500 grams Minced Beef

3 Tablespoons Ground Rice

½ Teaspoon Salt

½ Teaspoon Black Pepper

1 Tablespoon Olive Oil

1 Tablespoon Olive Oil

1 Large Onion

3 Cloves Garlic

1 Tablespoon Tomato Puree

5 Large Tomatoes

400ml Beef Stock

Juice of ½ a Lemon

1 Tablespoon Dried Oregano

¼ Teaspoon Ground Cinnamon

1 Teaspoon Sugar

½ Teaspoon Salt

½ Teaspoon Pepper

Water for Pasta

400 grams Tagliatelle

Garlic Bread

75 grams Butter

1 Teaspoon Garlic Puree

1 Teaspoon Oregano

Pinch of Black Pepper

6-8 Slices of Bread

NOTES;

The ground rice dries and binds the meatballs- breadcrumbs can be used.

Any pasta can be used.

Fresh, uncut bread is best for the garlic bread.

For a vegan option replace the beef for plant-based alternative and use a vegetable stock. Use plant-based butter.

Meatballs with Tagliatelle and Garlic Bread

A comfort dinner with a really easy garlic bread.
Serves 5

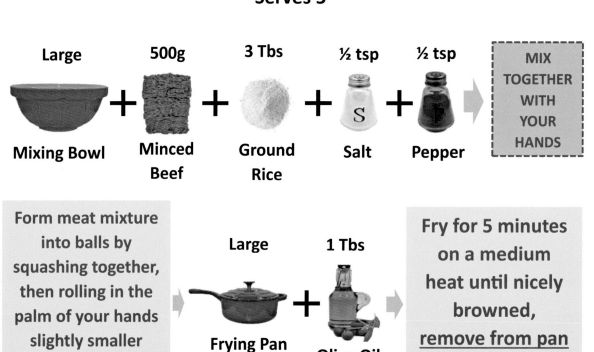

Large	500g	3 Tbs	½ tsp	½ tsp	MIX TOGETHER WITH YOUR HANDS
Mixing Bowl	Minced Beef	Ground Rice	Salt	Pepper	

Form meat mixture into balls by squashing together, then rolling in the palm of your hands slightly smaller than a golf ball in size, makes 12-14

Large — Frying Pan with Lid
1 Tbs — Olive Oil

Fry for 5 minutes on a medium heat until nicely browned, remove from pan and SET ASIDE

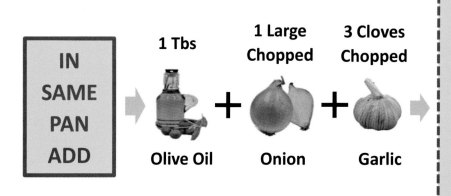

IN SAME PAN ADD

1 Tbs — Olive Oil
1 Large Chopped — Onion
3 Cloves Chopped — Garlic

Fry for 5 minutes until soft on a med/low heat stirring often ADD 4 Tbs of water during cooking

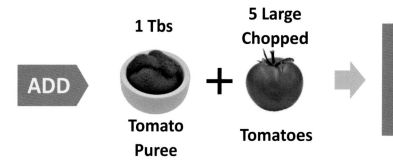

ADD

1 Tbs — Tomato Puree
5 Large Chopped — Tomatoes

Continue to cook for 5 minutes stirring regularly

ADD 400ml Beef Stock + Juice of ½ Lemon + 1 Tbs Dried Oregano + ¼ tsp Ground Cinnamon + 1 tsp Sugar

+ ½ tsp Salt + ½ tsp Pepper

Add the meatballs to the pot cover and cook on low heat for 20 minutes- adding a little water if necessary. **START PASTA**

Large Saucepan + ¾ Full Water

+ 400g Tagliatelle

Add pasta to boiling water, bring back to boiling point, simmer on medium heat for 10 minutes, then drain

Whilst pasta is cooking start the Garlic Bread

MIX 75g Softened Butter + 1 tsp Garlic Puree + 1 tsp Dried Oregano + Pinch Pepper **THEN TOAST** 6-8 Slices Sliced Bread

Spread butter mixture on toast

Bring meatballs and pasta together serve with garlic bread and grated cheese

YOUR NOTES

Vegan Moussaka

Ingredients

200 grams Split Red Lentils

375ml Water

1 Teaspoon Salt

2 Large Aubergines

2 Large Courgettes

2 Large Potatoes

4 Tablespoons Olive Oil

1 Teaspoons Salt

1 Tablespoon Olive Oil

1 Small Onion

2 Cloves Garlic

3 Large Tomatoes

1 Tablespoon Dried Oregano

¼ Teaspoon Ground Cinnamon

¼ Teaspoon Ground Nutmeg

½ Teaspoon Black Pepper

Juice of ½ Lemon

200ml Vegetable Stock

1 Teaspoon Sugar

3 Tablespoons Olive Oil

4 Tablespoons Plain Flour

500ml Oat/Soya Milk

1 Teaspoon Wholegrain Mustard

½ Teaspoon Salt

½ Teaspoon Black Pepper

½ Teaspoon Garlic Puree

1 Teaspoon Lemon Juice

NOTES;

Wash the lentils in the saucepan by filling and carefully emptying the water from the saucepan several times until the water is clear.

You may need to cook the vegetables in the oven in batches if there's not enough room in your oven.

Use a non-stick paper or foil if your trays are not non-stick.

Soya milk can be used for the white sauce.

If you don't have a large enough dish, use two smaller ones.

14

Vegan Moussaka

A delicious alternative to meat. Set oven to 180°c.

Serves 6

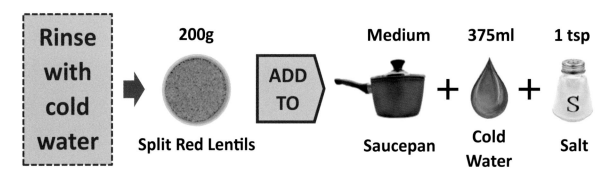

Rinse with cold water	200g	ADD TO	Medium	375ml	1 tsp
	Split Red Lentils		Saucepan	Cold Water	Salt

Bring the lentils to the boil, skim off scum and reduce to low heat and simmer for 10 minutes SET ASIDE

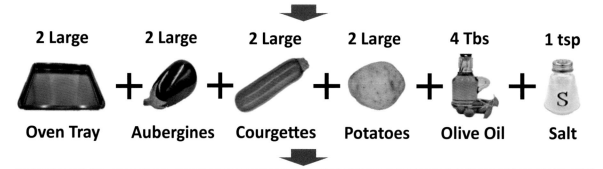

2 Large	2 Large	2 Large	2 Large	4 Tbs	1 tsp
Oven Tray	Aubergines	Courgettes	Potatoes	Olive Oil	Salt

Cut vegetables lengthways about 5mm thick. Then, with your hands, coat the vegetables in Olive Oil then lay out on tray- it doesn't matter if the vegetables overlap
Sprinkle salt on the aubergine only

BAKE IN OVEN FOR 20 MINUTES AT 180°c
DO NOT TURN VEGETABLES. WHEN COOKED SET ASIDE

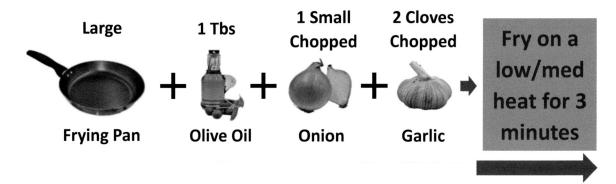

Large	1 Tbs	1 Small Chopped	2 Cloves Chopped	Fry on a low/med heat for 3 minutes
Frying Pan	Olive Oil	Onion	Garlic	

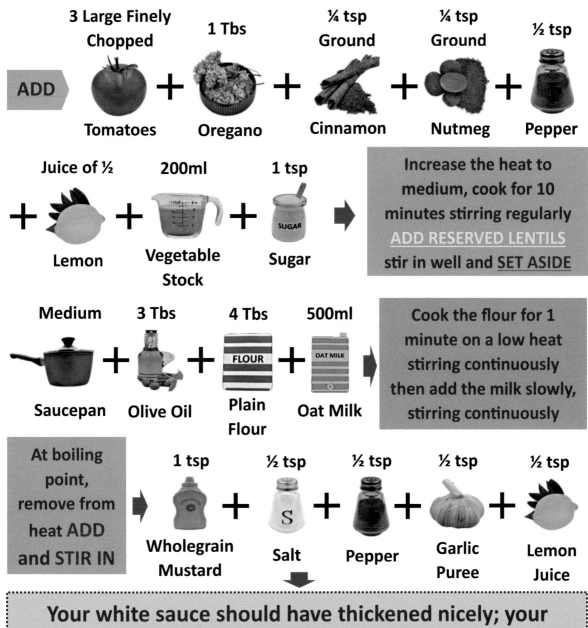

ADD

3 Large Finely Chopped **Tomatoes** + 1 Tbs **Oregano** + ¼ tsp Ground **Cinnamon** + ¼ tsp Ground **Nutmeg** + ½ tsp **Pepper**

+ Juice of ½ **Lemon** + 200ml **Vegetable Stock** + 1 tsp **Sugar**

Increase the heat to medium, cook for 10 minutes stirring regularly ADD RESERVED LENTILS stir in well and SET ASIDE

Medium **Saucepan** + 3 Tbs **Olive Oil** + 4 Tbs **Plain Flour** + 500ml **Oat Milk**

Cook the flour for 1 minute on a low heat stirring continuously then add the milk slowly, stirring continuously

At boiling point, remove from heat ADD and STIR IN

1 tsp **Wholegrain Mustard** + ½ tsp **Salt** + ½ tsp **Pepper** + ½ tsp **Garlic Puree** + ½ tsp **Lemon Juice**

Your white sauce should have thickened nicely; your sauce is now ready to use

Large Approximately 28cm x 22cm

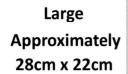

Roasting Dish

LAYER THE ROASTED VEGETABLES AND LENTIL MIXTURE; LENTILS, POTATO, LENTILS, COURGETTE, LENTILS, AUBERGINE, POUR OVER THE WHITE SAUCE, BAKE IN OVEN AT 180°C FOR 35 MINUTES, SERVE WITH CARROTS

Stuffed Peppers

Ingredients

1 Tablespoon Olive Oil

1 Red Pepper

1 Green Pepper

Water for Rice

150 grams Long Grain Rice

2 Tablespoons Olive Oil

½ Onion

2 Cloves Garlic

40 grams Mushrooms

40 grams Green Pepper

40 grams French Beans

40 grams Celery

½ Teaspoon Ground Cinnamon

2 Teaspoons Oregano

½ Teaspoon Salt

½ Teaspoon Black Pepper

1 Tablespoon Lemon Juice

50 grams Pine Nuts

3 Large Potatoes

1 Tin Chopped Tomatoes

1 Teaspoon Oregano

2 Tablespoons Olive Oil

2 Tablespoons Sugar

½ Teaspoon Black Pepper

½ Teaspoon Salt

1 Tablespoon Lemon Juice

NOTES;

You can use any vegetables or colour of peppers you desire in the rice mixture.

You can prepare this dish well in advance before baking in the oven.

The aubergine, courgette and other vegetables you have left over can be used for your next meal- a pasta sauce for example.

15

Stuffed Peppers

A Greek dish that takes you to Greece, you can include stuffed tomatoes.   Set oven to 180°c

Serves 4

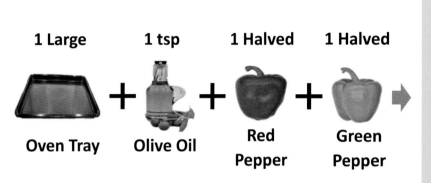

1 Large   **1 tsp**   **1 Halved**   **1 Halved**

Oven Tray   Olive Oil   Red Pepper   Green Pepper

De-seed the peppers, rub the oil over the skins, place cut side down on oven tray and bake for 10 minutes in the oven at 180°c **SET ASIDE**

Small   **¾ Full**   **150g**

Saucepan   Cold Water   Long Grain Rice

Bring water to boil, add rice and bring back to boil simmer for 10 minutes, drain **SET ASIDE**

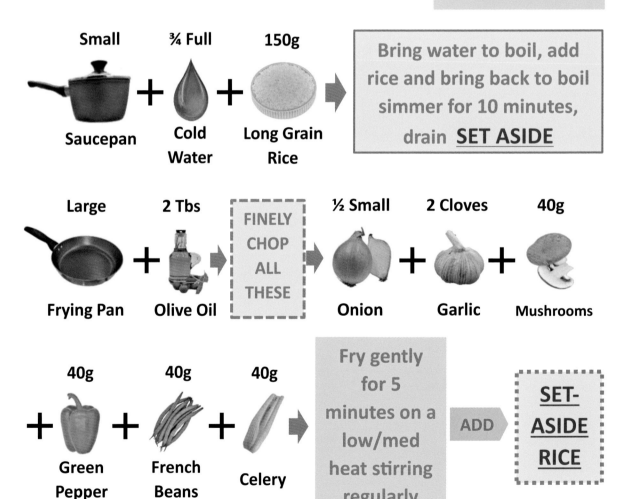

Large   **2 Tbs**   FINELY CHOP ALL THESE   **½ Small**   **2 Cloves**   **40g**

Frying Pan   Olive Oil   Onion   Garlic   Mushrooms

40g   **40g**   **40g**

Green Pepper   French Beans   Celery

Fry gently for 5 minutes on a low/med heat stirring regularly   ADD   **SET-ASIDE RICE**

½ tsp
Ground Cinnamon

+

2 tsp
Oregano

+

½ tsp
Salt

+

½ tsp
Pepper

+

1 Tbs
Lemon Juice

→

SET ASIDE

Small
Frying Pan

+

50g
Pine Nuts

→

Toast pine nuts in dry pan on a medium heat for 1-2 minutes until lightly browned **ADD TO RICE MIXTURE**

PLACE PEPPERS IN DISH

Large
Roasting Dish

Fill the halved peppers with the **rice mixture**

→

3 Large
Peeled Potatoes

→

Cut potatoes into wedges, fill the space around the peppers with the wedges **SET ASIDE**

500ml
Jug

+

1 Tin (400g) Chopped
Tomatoes

+

1 tsp
Oregano

+

2 Tbs
Olive Oil

+

2 Tbs
Sugar

+

½ tsp
Pepper

+

½ tsp
Salt

+

1 Tbs
Lemon Juice

↓

POUR THE TOMATO MIXTURE OVER THE POTATOES THEN ROAST IN THE OVEN AT 180°C FOR 40 MINUTES **SERVE**

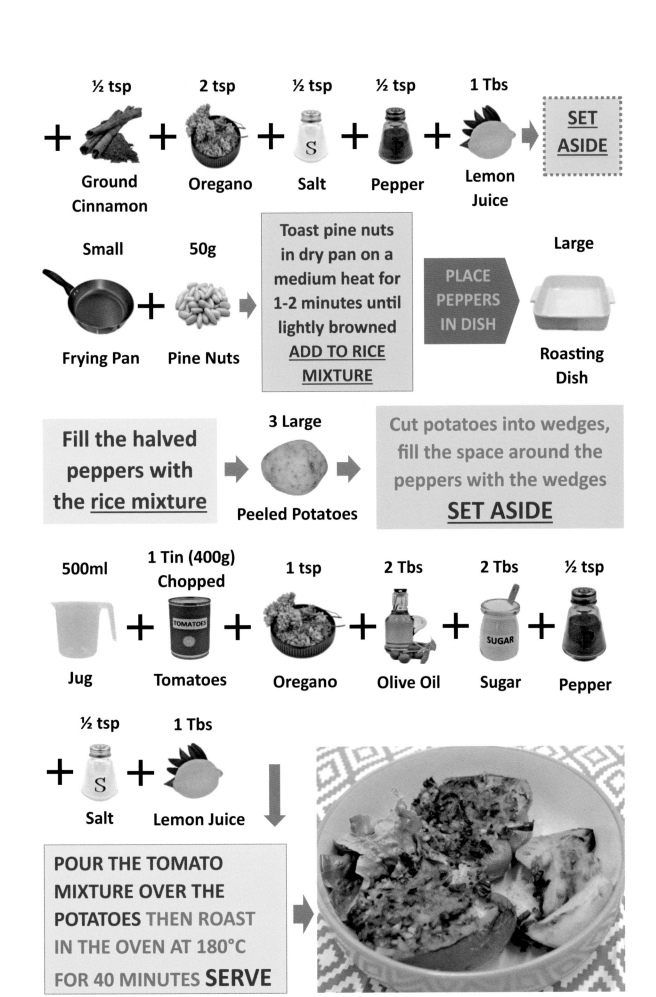

Tuna and Butter Bean Pasta Bake

Ingredients

Water for Pasta

350 grams Penne Pasta

3 Tablespoons Olive Oil

1 Large Onion

4 Cloves Garlic

1 Tablespoon Oregano

½ Teaspoon Black Pepper

3 Tablespoons Water

5 Large Tomatoes

1 Tablespoon Tomato Puree

1 Tablespoon Sugar

1 Teaspoon Salt

Juice of ½ a Lemon

350ml Water

2 Tablespoons Corn Flour

2 Tins Tuna (220g Drained)

1 Tin Butter Beans (400g Drained)

10 grams Fresh Basil

250 grams Medium Cheddar

Drizzle of Olive Oil

Grinding of Black Pepper

NOTES;

You can use any short pasta for this dish.

Any type of pulse can be used.

Any cheddar cheese of your preference can be used.

For a vegan option replace the tuna with Black Olives, and use a plant-based cheese alternative.

Tuna and Butter Bean Pasta Bake

Delicious, quick and easy meal for hungry people.
Set oven to 220°c   Serves 6

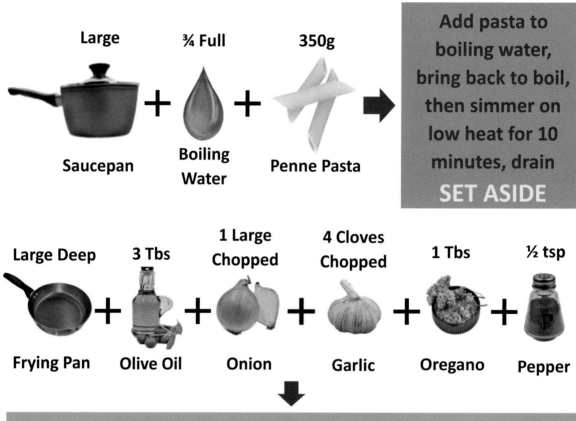

Large	¾ Full	350g
Saucepan	Boiling Water	Penne Pasta

Add pasta to boiling water, bring back to boil, then simmer on low heat for 10 minutes, drain SET ASIDE

Large Deep	3 Tbs	1 Large Chopped	4 Cloves Chopped	1 Tbs	½ tsp
Frying Pan	Olive Oil	Onion	Garlic	Oregano	Pepper

Fry on a med/low heat for 5 minutes stirring continually, halfway through ADD 3 TABLESPOONS OF WATER

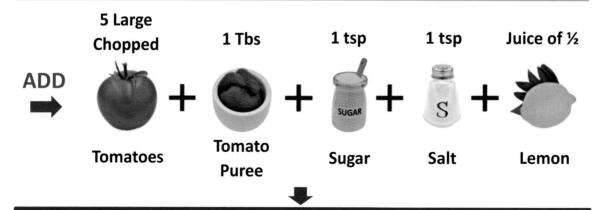

ADD

5 Large Chopped	1 Tbs	1 tsp	1 tsp	Juice of ½
Tomatoes	Tomato Puree	Sugar	Salt	Lemon

Cook for a further 5 minutes on a medium heat stirring regularly

Large | 350ml | 2 Tbs

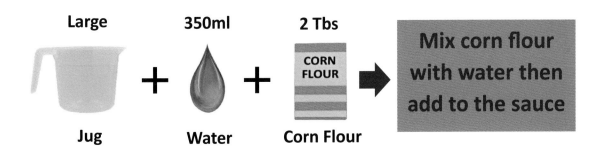

Jug + Water + Corn Flour → Mix corn flour with water then add to the sauce

2 Tins (220g) Drained | 1 Tin (400g) | 10g Chopped

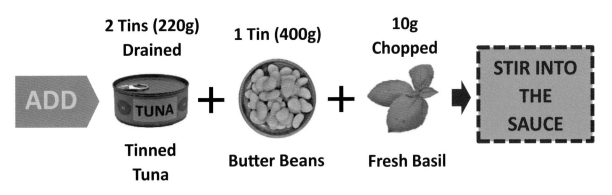

ADD ▶ Tinned Tuna + Butter Beans + Fresh Basil → STIR INTO THE SAUCE

Large | 250g Grated

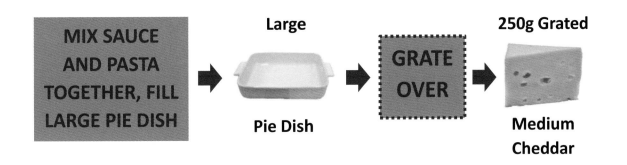

MIX SAUCE AND PASTA TOGETHER, FILL LARGE PIE DISH → Pie Dish → GRATE OVER → Medium Cheddar

DRIZZLE OVER OLIVE OIL ➡

GRIND OVER PEPPER ➡

BAKE IN THE OVEN FOR 15 MINUTES AT 220°C

SERVE ➡

Spanish Paella
Ingredients

3 Tablespoons Olive Oil

1 Large Onion

5 Cloves Garlic

150 grams Chorizo Sausage

450 grams Cubed Chicken

350 grams Arborio Rice

400ml Chicken Stock

400ml Water

1 Teaspoon Salt

1 Teaspoon Black Pepper

½ Teaspoon Sweet/Mild Paprika

8 Strands Saffron

1 Red Pepper

Juice of ½ Lemon

200 grams Peas

2 Large Tomatoes

250 grams Raw King Prawns

20 grams Flat Leaf Parsley

2 Lemons

NOTES;

If after adding the prawns (the last 5 minutes of cooking) the rice is sticking to the pan, add a little water.

Making sure that the heat has been turned off, lay a tea towel over the foil to retain the heat.

Chicken drumsticks or thighs can be used, fry these first for 10 minutes.

Risotto or paella rice can be used.

Spanish Paella

A very filling dish that's really easy to cook and many variations can be made. A paella pan 38cm is ideal or a very large frying pan can be used. Serves 6

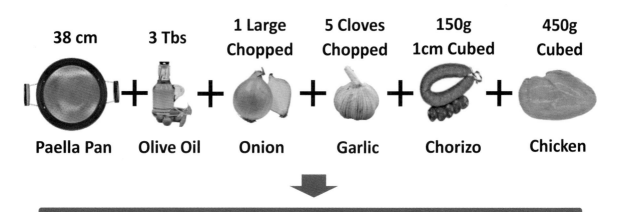

38 cm	3 Tbs	1 Large Chopped	5 Cloves Chopped	150g 1cm Cubed	450g Cubed
Paella Pan	Olive Oil	Onion	Garlic	Chorizo	Chicken

Fry for 5 minutes on a med/high heat, stirring continuously

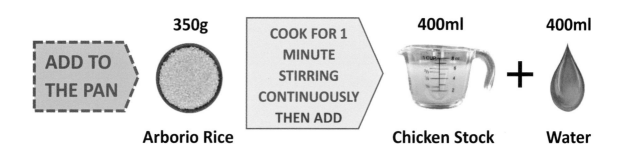

	350g	COOK FOR 1 MINUTE STIRRING CONTINUOUSLY THEN ADD	400ml	400ml
ADD TO THE PAN	Arborio Rice		Chicken Stock	Water

	1 tsp	1 tsp	½ tsp	8 Strands	1 Sliced	Juice of ½
ADD	Salt	Pepper	Sweet Paprika	Saffron	Red Pepper	Lemon

Cook on a medium heat for 15 minutes, stir occasionally

ADD TO THE PAN

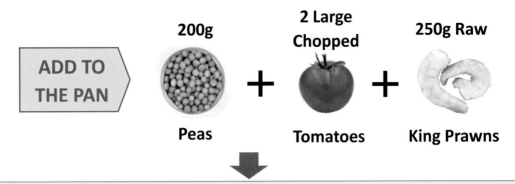

200g
Peas

2 Large Chopped
Tomatoes

250g Raw
King Prawns

Stir in and cook for 5 minutes on a low/med heat, stir once or twice and add some water if too dry

Turn off heat and cover with foil.
Leave to stand for 10 minutes

Uncover, stir, then garnish the pan with

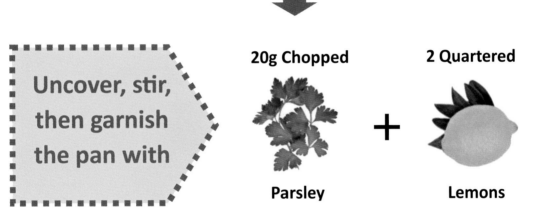

20g Chopped
Parsley

2 Quartered
Lemons

Place the quartered lemons around the edge of pan, sprinkle with the parsley

SERVE

King Prawn Linguine

Ingredients

Water for Pasta

350 grams Linguine

1 Tablespoon Olive Oil

30 grams Butter

1 Large Onion

4 Cloves Garlic

2 Medium Tomatoes

2 Teaspoons Oregano

2 Teaspoons Tomato Puree

½ Teaspoon Salt

½ Teaspoon Black Pepper

2 Teaspoons sugar

Juice ½ Lemon

400 grams Raw King Prawns

NOTES;

If at any point the sauce starts to burn, add a little water.

Any pasta can be used.

Apart from the prawns this is a basic pasta sauce and any ingredient can be used to make whatever sauce you desire.

For a vegan option replace king prawns with butter beans.

King Prawn Linguine

Simple, Light and Delicious.   Serves 4

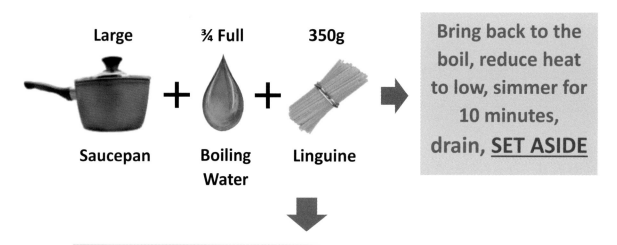

Large	¾ Full	350g	Bring back to the boil, reduce heat to low, simmer for 10 minutes, drain, **SET ASIDE**
Saucepan	Boiling Water	Linguine	

 ## While pasta is cooking, cook the sauce

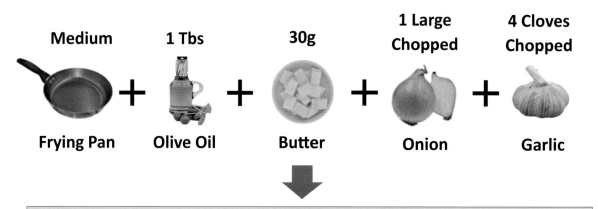

Medium	1 Tbs	30g	1 Large Chopped	4 Cloves Chopped
Frying Pan	Olive Oil	Butter	Onion	Garlic

Fry on a medium heat for 5 minutes stirring continuously

ADD TO THE PAN	2 Medium Chopped	2 tsp	2 tsp	Cook for 3 more minutes
	Tomatoes	Oregano	Tomato Puree	

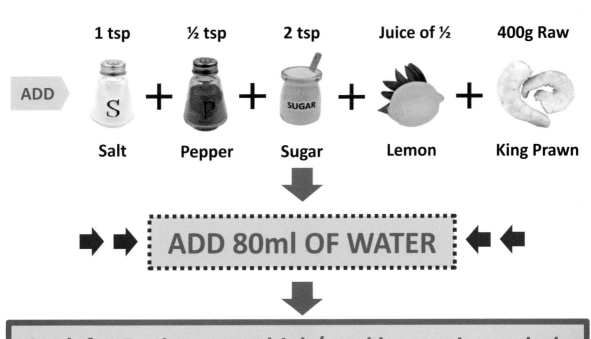

ADD | 1 tsp **Salt** + ½ tsp **Pepper** + 2 tsp **Sugar** + Juice of ½ **Lemon** + 400g Raw **King Prawn**

ADD 80ml OF WATER

Cook for 5 minutes on high/med heat, stir regularly

MIX SAUCE WITH LINGUINE

GRATE ON CHEESE IF YOU LIKE

SERVE

Cao Lau

Ingredients

750 grams Thick Pork Chops

8 Cloves Garlic

2 Teaspoons Ground Five Spice

100ml Light Soy Sauce

4 Tablespoons Sugar

½ Teaspoon Salt

1 Teaspoon Black Pepper

300ml Water for Stock

1 Onion

6 Whole Cloves

100ml Vegetable Oil

250 grams Cos Lettuce

30 grams Coriander

30 grams Thai Basil

20 grams Mint

100 grams Baby Leaf Spinach

Water For Noodles

400 grams Wholewheat Noodles

NOTES;

Buy thick pork chops with the bone in- if unavailable you can replace stock with water instead of making a stock.

Pork loin can be used.

Try different combinations of salad leaf.

Try different noodles.

You can mix the salad leaves and noodles together placing the sliced pork on top before serving.

Try adding some crushed roasted peanuts as well.

For a vegan alternative use Tofu and a vegetable stock.

Cao Lau

A Vietnamese dish, my kids love this.   Serves 6

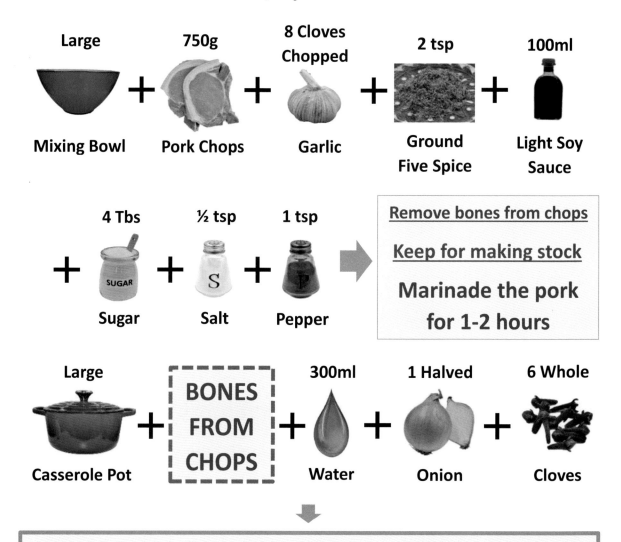

Large — Mixing Bowl
+
750g — Pork Chops
+
8 Cloves Chopped — Garlic
+
2 tsp — Ground Five Spice
+
100ml — Light Soy Sauce

+
4 Tbs — Sugar
+
½ tsp — Salt
+
1 tsp — Pepper
→

Remove bones from chops

Keep for making stock

Marinade the pork for 1-2 hours

Large — Casserole Pot
+
BONES FROM CHOPS
+
300ml — Water
+
1 Halved — Onion
+
6 Whole — Cloves

Bring to the boil, reduce heat to low, simmer for 40 minutes, use a sieve to remove onion and cloves from the stock SET ASIDE

Large — Casserole Pot
+
100ml — Veg Oil
→

Shake off marinade from chops. Then, fry the chops in oil for 5 minutes on medium heat, turning once until well - browned

DRAIN OFF THE OIL AND ADD ½ THE MARINADE AND 50ML OF THE STOCK

→

COVER THE POT AND PLACE IN THE OVEN AT 200°C FOR 45 MINUTES

→

ADD THE REST OF THE MARINADE AND 150ML OF STOCK. CONTINUE TO COOK IN OVEN FOR A FURTHER 45 MINUTES

↓

WHILE MEAT IS COOKING PREPARE SALAD LEAVES

↓

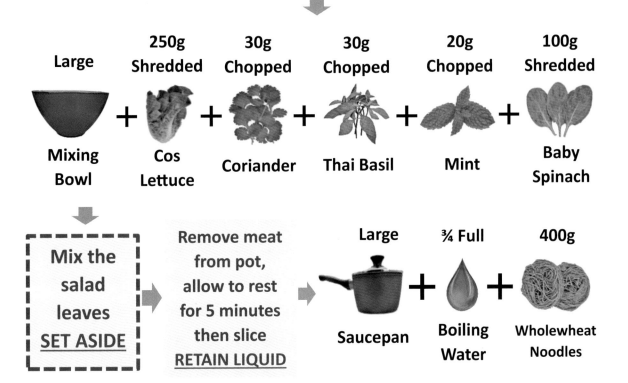

Large — Mixing Bowl + 250g Shredded — Cos Lettuce + 30g Chopped — Coriander + 30g Chopped — Thai Basil + 20g Chopped — Mint + 100g Shredded — Baby Spinach

↓

Mix the salad leaves SET ASIDE

→

Remove meat from pot, allow to rest for 5 minutes then slice RETAIN LIQUID

→

Large — Saucepan + ¾ Full — Boiling Water + 400g — Wholewheat Noodles

↓

Drop noodles in boiling water, simmer for 5 minutes, drain THEN ADD RETAINED LIQUID from the meat to the noodles

→

SERVE in separate bowls the meat, salad and noodles

Mix together at the table to your own liking

→

YOUR NOTES

Fajitas

Ingredients

750 grams Chicken Breast

1 Tablespoon Olive Oil

2 Tablespoons Ground Cinnamon

2 Tablespoons Ground Coriander

2 Tablespoons Ground Cumin

2 Tablespoons Ground Ginger

2 Tablespoons Ground Chilli

1 Teaspoon Dried Thyme

1 Teaspoon Salt

2 Teaspoons Black pepper

Juice of ½ a Lemon

4 Large Tomatoes

1 Whole Cucumber

1 Bunch Spring Onions

Juice of ½ a Lemon

1 Large or 2 Small Avocados

½ Teaspoon Garlic Puree

Pinch Salt

Pinch Pepper

1 Teaspoon Lemon Juice

1 Tablespoon Olive Oil

2 Medium Onions

4 Cloves Garlic

1 Red Pepper

1 Green Pepper

12 Large Tortilla Wraps

300ml Sour Cream

250 grams Cheddar Cheese

215-gram Jar Jalapeños

NOTES;

Don't fill you Tortillas too much or they will be difficult to wrap.

You can fry your chicken mixture instead of roasting.

I've allowed two Tortillas each for adult portions, kids may only need one.

Any leftovers can be used for packed lunch or even a sandwich.

For vegan option replace dairy ingredients with plant-based alternative and replace chicken with soya chunks.

20

Fajitas

Great for serving at the table, building your own wrap is fun- especially for the kids.   Set oven to 220°c   Serves 6

Large — Mixing Bowl + 750g Cubed — Chicken Breast + 1 Tbs — Olive Oil + 2 tsp — Ground Cinnamon + 2 tsp — Ground Coriander + 2 tsp — Ground Cumin

+ 2 tsp — Ground Ginger + 2 tsp — Ground Chilli + 1 tsp — Dried Thyme + 1 tsp — Salt + 2 tsp — Pepper + Juice of ½ — Lemon

Mix together leave covered for at least 1 hour

FINELY CHOP THE SALAD INGREDIENTS

Medium — Bowl + 4 Large — Tomatoes

+ 1 Whole — Cucumber + 1 Bunch — Spring Onions + Juice of ½ — Lemon

MIX TOGETHER THEN SET ASIDE

Make the guacamole - mash the avocado first

Medium — Bowl + 1 Large — Avocado + ½ tsp — Garlic Puree + Pinch — Salt

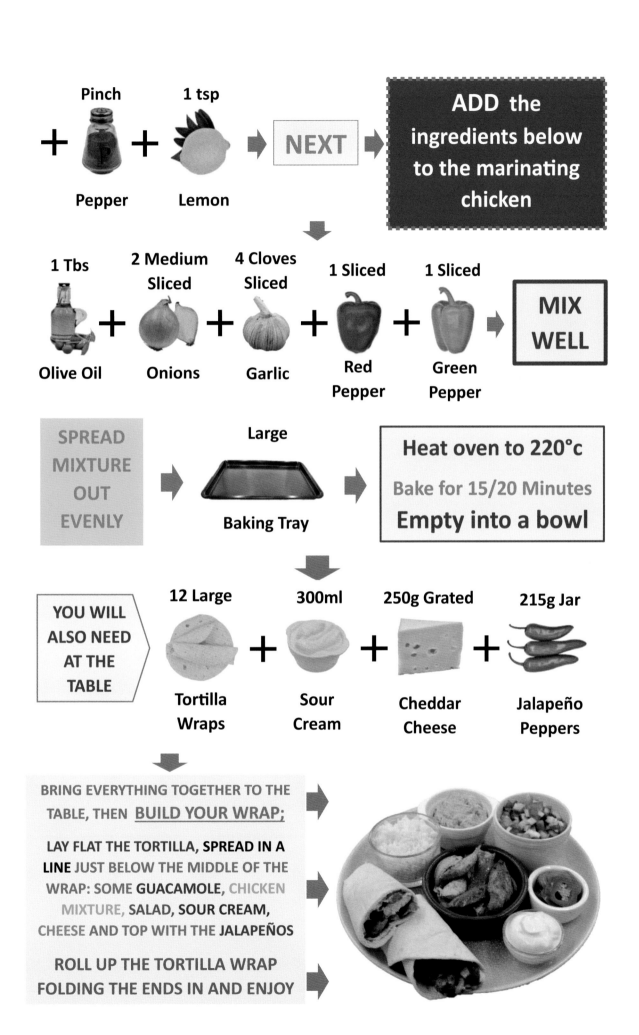

Pinch
Pepper

1 tsp
Lemon

NEXT

ADD the ingredients below to the marinating chicken

1 Tbs
Olive Oil

2 Medium Sliced
Onions

4 Cloves Sliced
Garlic

1 Sliced
Red Pepper

1 Sliced
Green Pepper

MIX WELL

SPREAD MIXTURE OUT EVENLY

Large
Baking Tray

Heat oven to 220°c

Bake for 15/20 Minutes

Empty into a bowl

YOU WILL ALSO NEED AT THE TABLE

12 Large
Tortilla Wraps

300ml
Sour Cream

250g Grated
Cheddar Cheese

215g Jar
Jalapeño Peppers

BRING EVERYTHING TOGETHER TO THE TABLE, THEN **BUILD YOUR WRAP;**

LAY FLAT THE TORTILLA, **SPREAD IN A LINE** JUST BELOW THE MIDDLE OF THE WRAP: SOME **GUACAMOLE**, CHICKEN MIXTURE, **SALAD, SOUR CREAM,** CHEESE AND TOP WITH THE **JALAPEÑOS**

ROLL UP THE TORTILLA WRAP FOLDING THE ENDS IN AND ENJOY

Lasagne

Ingredients

1 Tablespoon Olive Oil

1 Large Onion

3 Cloves Garlic

2 Teaspoons Oregano

5 Large Tomatoes

Juice of ½ a Lemon

350ml Beef Stock

½ Teaspoon Ground Cinnamon

1 Teaspoon Salt

½ Teaspoon Black Pepper

1 Tablespoon Olive Oil

750 grams Minced Beef

5 Tablespoons Vegetable Oil

100 grams Plain Flour

1 Litre Whole Milk

1 Teaspoon Dijon Mustard

¼ Teaspoon Ground Nutmeg

½ Teaspoon Salt

½ Teaspoon Black Pepper

180 grams Pasta Sheets

1 Sliced Tomato

Drizzle of Olive Oil

NOTES;

For a vegan option use soya or oat milk, a 50-50 combination works well, replace the meat with plant-based mince or puy lentils and use vegetable stock.

You can use individual pie dishes if you like and freeze some for another day.

Finely chopped carrots and celery can be added to the first stage for a different deeper flavour.

Add a little more water to the beef and tomato mixture if needed.

Lasagne

Great, comforting, family meal.

Set oven to 180°c   Serves 6

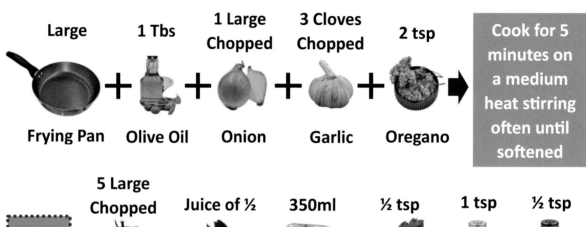

Large — Frying Pan
+ **1 Tbs** — Olive Oil
+ **1 Large Chopped** — Onion
+ **3 Cloves Chopped** — Garlic
+ **2 tsp** — Oregano
➡ Cook for 5 minutes on a medium heat stirring often until softened

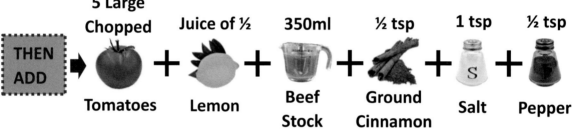

THEN ADD ➡ **5 Large Chopped** — Tomatoes
+ **Juice of ½** — Lemon
+ **350ml** — Beef Stock
+ **½ tsp** — Ground Cinnamon
+ **1 tsp** — Salt
+ **½ tsp** — Pepper

Cook for 5 more minutes on a med/high heat, stir often

REMOVE FROM PAN ➡ SET ASIDE ➡ USING THE SAME PAN

ADD **1 Tbs** — Olive Oil
+ **750g** — Minced Beef
➡ Cook on a high heat for 6 minutes, stirring regularly until well-browned
➡ ADD THE TOMATO SAUCE MIXTURE BACK TO THE PAN, COOK FOR 5 MINUTES
SET ASIDE

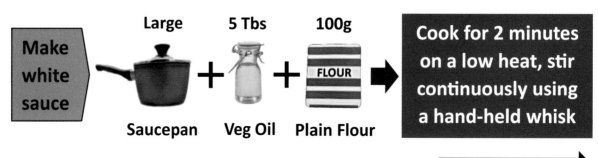

Make white sauce **Large** — Saucepan
+ **5 Tbs** — Veg Oil
+ **100g** — Plain Flour
➡ Cook for 2 minutes on a low heat, stir continuously using a hand-held whisk

➡

21

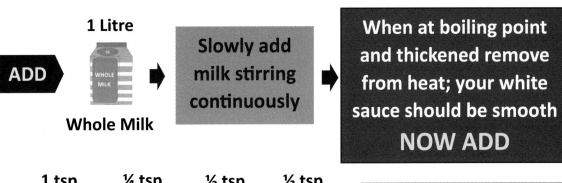

ADD → 1 Litre / Whole Milk → Slowly add milk stirring continuously → When at boiling point and thickened remove from heat; your white sauce should be smooth **NOW ADD**

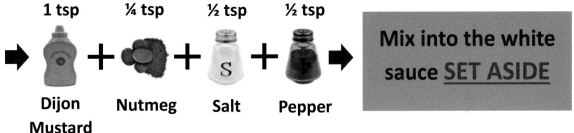

→ 1 tsp **Dijon Mustard** + ¼ tsp **Nutmeg** + ½ tsp **Salt** + ½ tsp **Pepper** → Mix into the white sauce **SET ASIDE**

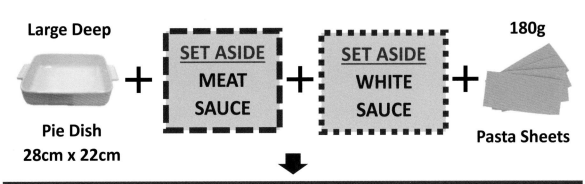

Large Deep Pie Dish 28cm x 22cm + SET ASIDE **MEAT SAUCE** + SET ASIDE **WHITE SAUCE** + 180g **Pasta Sheets**

↓

Roughly divide both the meat and white sauce mixtures into thirds
First meat then white sauce then a layer of pasta sheets
REPEAT Finish with a layer of meat then white sauce

PLACE ON TOP, SLICES OF TOMATO AND DRIZZLE WITH OLIVE OIL

BAKE FOR 30 MINUTES AT 180°C

SERVE WITH A SALAD OF YOUR CHOICE or CARROTS AND BROCCOLI

→

Salmon Ramen
Ingredients

120 grams Sugar

100ml Light Soy Sauce

1 Tablespoon Dark Soy Sauce

2 Tablespoons Mirin

2 Tablespoons Sake

400ml Chicken Stock

1.4 Litres Water

80 grams White Miso Paste

¼ Tsp White Pepper

3 Tablespoons Vegetable Oil

480 grams Salmon Fillets

2 Heads Pak Choi

1 Red Pepper

150 grams Button Mushrooms

5 Spring Onions

Water for Noodles

350 grams Wholewheat Noodles

100 grams Lambs Lettuce

NOTES;

After pouring the teriyaki sauce onto the salmon, the sauce should bubble and thicken within 2 minutes.

Any type of noodle can be used.

You can cook the noodles in the stock if you prefer.

You can use any type of vegetable you like.

You can use chicken, beef, tofu or pork- even slices of sweet potato.

Any leftover teriyaki can be stored for at least a week.

Naturally-brewed soy sauce is best.

Cheap Sake and Mirin are fine to use.

Spinach could be used as a replacement for the lambs lettuce.

Salmon Ramen

Lovely dish, full of flavour; the Teriyaki sauce really makes this dish.   **Serves 4**

Small	120g	100ml	1 Tbs	2 Tbs	2Tbs
Saucepan	Sugar	Light Soy Sauce	Dark Soy Sauce	Mirin	Sake

Dissolve the sugar gently for 5-6 minutes on a low/med heat stirring continuously, remove from heat   <u>SET ASIDE</u>

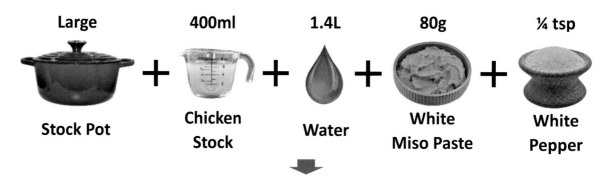

Large	400ml	1.4L	80g	¼ tsp
Stock Pot	Chicken Stock	Water	White Miso Paste	White Pepper

Heat the broth to dissolve the miso paste, keep the broth hot until your ready to put in your vegetables

Remove the skin from the Salmon Fillet

Remove the skin by placing the fish on a flat surface skin-side down. With a large, sharp knife cut in between the meat and skin - as close to the skin as possible. Keeping your knife flat to the surface, apply slight downward pressure and pull the knife through the length of the fillet.

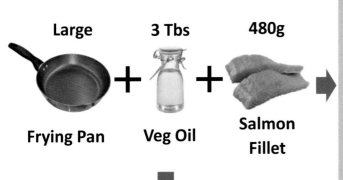

Large
Frying Pan

+

3 Tbs
Veg Oil

+

480g
Salmon Fillet

→

Cook on a med/low heat for 6-8 minutes, turning half way through then pour away oil and ADD the <u>SET ASIDE</u> Teriyaki sauce, turn up the heat to med/low cook for 2 minutes turning once, remove from heat, now ready to serve

WHILE THE SALMON IS COOKING ADD TO THE <u>STOCK POT</u>:

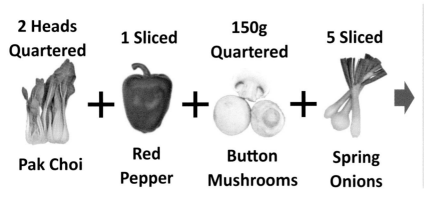

2 Heads Quartered
Pak Choi

+

1 Sliced
Red Pepper

+

150g Quartered
Button Mushrooms

+

5 Sliced
Spring Onions

→

Bring stockpot up to boiling point, reduce heat to low and cook for 5 minutes. Then remove from heat until needed

After adding the vegetables to the stockpot <u>START YOUR</u> NOODLES

→

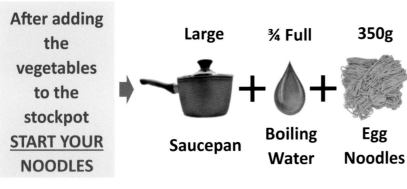

Large
Saucepan

+

¾ Full
Boiling Water

+

350g
Egg Noodles

→

Bring back to the boil, turn off the heat and leave for 5 minutes, drain

BUILD YOUR DISH   <u>DIVIDE BY FOUR</u>

In large bowls put in the noodles

Ladle over stock and vegetables

100 grams of lambs lettuce →

Place the fish on top

Drizzle with teriyaki sauce

➡ **SERVE** ➡

Pizza Neapolitan

Ingredients

500 grams Strong Bread Flour

2 Teaspoons Olive Oil

½ Teaspoon Salt

½ Teaspoon Sugar

7 grams Fast Acting Dried Yeast

330ml Warm Water

1 Tablespoon Olive Oil

1 Small Onion

2 Cloves Garlic

3 Large Tomatoes

1 Tablespoon Tomato Puree

½ Teaspoon Salt

¼ Teaspoon Black Pepper

1 Teaspoon Oregano

1 Teaspoon Lemon Juice

½ Teaspoon Sugar

50ml Water

180 grams Mozzarella

1 Medium Onion

1 Red Pepper

200 grams Cheddar Cheese

140 Grams Black Olives

A Handful Basil Leaves

A Drizzle of Olive Oil

NOTES;

The time spent kneading the dough is important to ensure a good rise of the dough, any technique is fine as long as you're stretching and folding the dough.

I use an oiled plate to cover the dough you can use oiled cling film or a damp tea-towel instead.

You can put any toppings you like on your pizza, be sure not to put to many toppings on or it will not cook properly.

A very hot oven will cook your pizza best.

Chips are a good accompaniment.

Pizza Neapolitan

Everyone loves pizza, and making the dough is easy.
Set oven to highest temperature at least 220°c   Makes 4

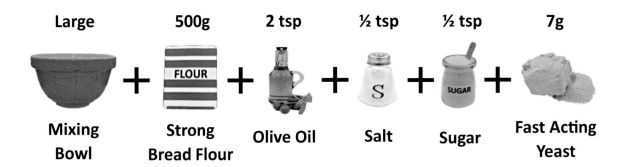

Large	500g	2 tsp	½ tsp	½ tsp	7g
Mixing Bowl	Strong Bread Flour	Olive Oil	Salt	Sugar	Fast Acting Yeast

330ml

Warm Water

Put the ingredients in the bowl, keeping the yeast and salt apart. Add most of the water and mix with one hand until a dough is formed, your dough should be together in a lump and slightly sticky. Add a little water if needed.

Turn out onto a floured or oiled surface and knead by stretching: with the heal of your hand push down and away from yourself and then bringing the dough back to the middle, Repeat this for at least 5 minutes. Your dough should be smooth and not sticky.

Now prove the dough by placing in a well-oiled bowl and covering with an oiled plate, leaving for 1-2 hours. When doubled in size, remove from bowl and on a floured surface knead for 10 seconds. Then, divide the dough into 4 parts, form into balls and roll out to your desired thickness.

While the dough is proving make the tomato sauce

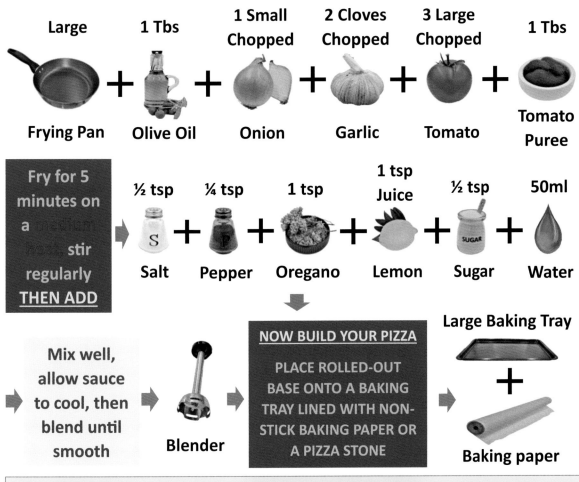

Large + 1 Tbs + 1 Small Chopped + 2 Cloves Chopped + 3 Large Chopped + 1 Tbs

Frying Pan | Olive Oil | Onion | Garlic | Tomato | Tomato Puree

Fry for 5 minutes on a medium heat, stir regularly THEN ADD

½ tsp + ¼ tsp + 1 tsp + 1 tsp Juice + ½ tsp + 50ml

Salt | Pepper | Oregano | Lemon | Sugar | Water

Mix well, allow sauce to cool, then blend until smooth → Blender →

NOW BUILD YOUR PIZZA

PLACE ROLLED-OUT BASE ONTO A BAKING TRAY LINED WITH NON-STICK BAKING PAPER OR A PIZZA STONE

Large Baking Tray + Baking paper

⬇ DIVIDE INGREDIENTS BELOW BY FOUR ⬇

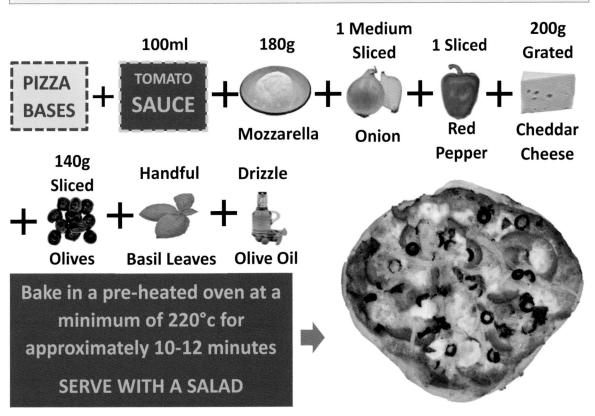

PIZZA BASES + 100ml TOMATO SAUCE + 180g Mozzarella + 1 Medium Sliced Onion + 1 Sliced Red Pepper + 200g Grated Cheddar Cheese

+ 140g Sliced Olives + Handful Basil Leaves + Drizzle Olive Oil

Bake in a pre-heated oven at a minimum of 220°c for approximately 10-12 minutes

SERVE WITH A SALAD

Beef Rendang

Ingredients

1 Tablespoon Coriander Seeds

1 Tablespoon Cumin Seeds

75 grams Desiccated Coconut

50ml Water

1 Tablespoon Dark Soy Sauce

½ Teaspoon Salt

3 Shallots

4 Cloves Garlic

1 or 2 Fresh Chillies

15 grams Fresh Ginger

3 Kaffir Lime Leaves

1 Stem of Lemongrass

2 Tablespoons Vegetable Oil

600 grams Beef

200ml Water

400ml Coconut Milk

1 Tablespoon Lime Juice

600ml Water for Rice

300 grams Basmati Rice

Small handful of Coriander

NOTES;

Good quality meat is best, Chuck or Brisket.

If you're not using a blender then a mortar and pestle could be used.

Use mild or hot chillies, whatever your preference.

For vegan option use chickpeas, and add along with the coconut milk.

Beef Rendang

Delicious curry! The long cooking process is well worth the wait and it's still easy to make.   Serves 4

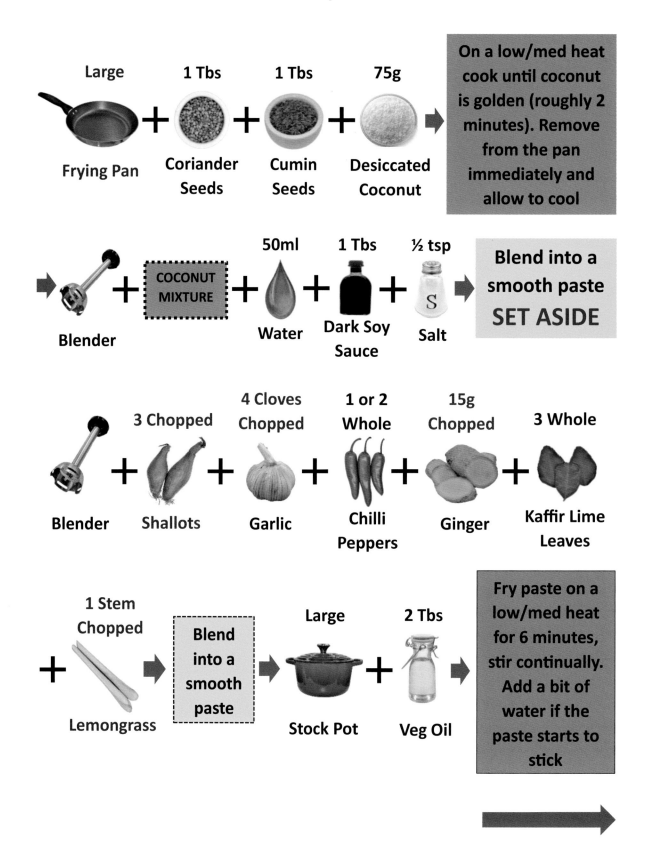

Large **+** 1 Tbs **+** 1 Tbs **+** 75g **→**

Frying Pan   Coriander Seeds   Cumin Seeds   Desiccated Coconut

On a low/med heat cook until coconut is golden (roughly 2 minutes). Remove from the pan immediately and allow to cool

→ Blender **+** COCONUT MIXTURE **+** 50ml **+** 1 Tbs **+** ½ tsp **→**

Water   Dark Soy Sauce   Salt

Blend into a smooth paste **SET ASIDE**

Blender **+** 3 Chopped Shallots **+** 4 Cloves Chopped Garlic **+** 1 or 2 Whole Chilli Peppers **+** 15g Chopped Ginger **+** 3 Whole Kaffir Lime Leaves

+ 1 Stem Chopped Lemongrass **→** Blend into a smooth paste **→** Large Stock Pot **+** 2 Tbs Veg Oil **→**

Fry paste on a low/med heat for 6 minutes, stir continually. Add a bit of water if the paste starts to stick

→

ADD

600g Cubed

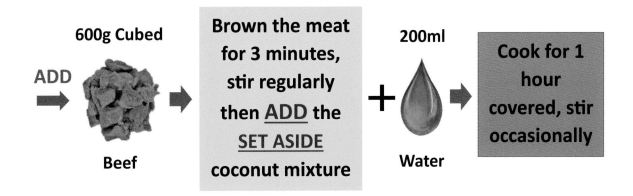

Beef

Brown the meat for 3 minutes, stir regularly then ADD the SET ASIDE coconut mixture

+

200ml

Water

Cook for 1 hour covered, stir occasionally

THEN ADD TO THE POT

400ml

Coconut Milk

+

1 Tbs Juice

Lime

Cook for 30 minutes covered

While the meat is cooking start the rice

Medium

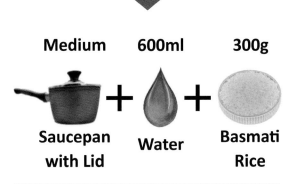

Saucepan with Lid

+

600ml

Water

+

300g

Basmati Rice

Sprinkle over some fresh coriander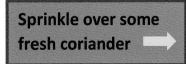

Bring to the boil, cover, reduce heat to lowest, cook for 5 minutes then turn off heat and leave to stand for at least 10 minutes

Burger and Chips

Ingredients

1 Tablespoon Olive Oil

350 grams Strong White Bread Flour

1 Teaspoon Salt

1 Teaspoon Sugar

240ml Warm Water

7 grams Fast-Acting Yeast

Water for Potatoes

900 grams Potatoes

675 grams Minced Beef

60 grams Fresh Breadcrumbs

½ Teaspoon Salt

½ Teaspoon Black Pepper

1 Teaspoon Olive Oil

Water for Sweetcorn

Lettuce, Tomatoes and Onions for Burger Filling

NOTES;

Burger baps can be brought if you do not want to make the baps yourself.

Working the dough is important. Knead for at least 5 minutes, any style of kneading is ok, stretching the dough is the key.

Before the 2nd rise, wet the top of the bun and dab in seeds if you want a seeded bun.

To make breadcrumbs toast a slice of bread, allow it to cool completely, then grate or blitz in a food processor into crumb.

For vegan option use plant-based burgers or boil some puy lentils in vegetable stock, drain, mash when cooled, mash butter beans, mix all together with breadcrumbs and seasonings, and form into a patty.

Burger and Chips

Making the rolls yourself takes the burgers to another level.

Set oven to 220°c   Makes 6

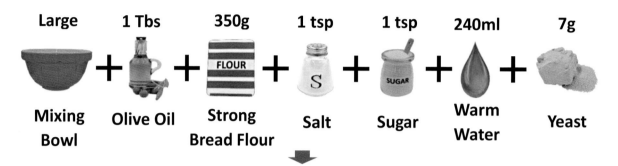

Large	1 Tbs	350g	1 tsp	1 tsp	240ml	7g
Mixing Bowl	Olive Oil	Strong Bread Flour	Salt	Sugar	Warm Water	Yeast

Put the ingredients in the bowl keeping the yeast and salt **apart**. Add most of the warm water, mixing with one hand until a dough is formed, adding some of the left-over water if needed. Your dough should be slightly sticky.

Turn out onto a floured surface and knead by stretching: with the heal of your hand push down and away from yourself and then bringing the dough back to the middle, repeat this for at least 5-10 minutes. Your dough should smooth and not sticky.

Prove the dough by placing in an oiled bowl and covering with an oiled plate for **1-2 hours,** when doubled in size remove from bowl. On a floured surface knead for 10 seconds then divide into 6 parts, form into balls tucking in at the bottom with your fingers until the upper part of the dough ball is smooth. Place the dough balls on non-stick paper, on a baking tray, cover with oiled cling-film and leave to rise for **1 hour** until doubled in size.

Once doubled in size bake in a hot oven at 220°c for 15 minutes. Place a tray of water at the bottom of the oven for a nice crust. Allow to cool before using.

WHILST THE DOUGH IS PROVING MAKE THE BEEF PATTIES AND CHIPS

START COOKING THE CHIPS ONCE THE BUNS ARE REMOVED FROM OVEN

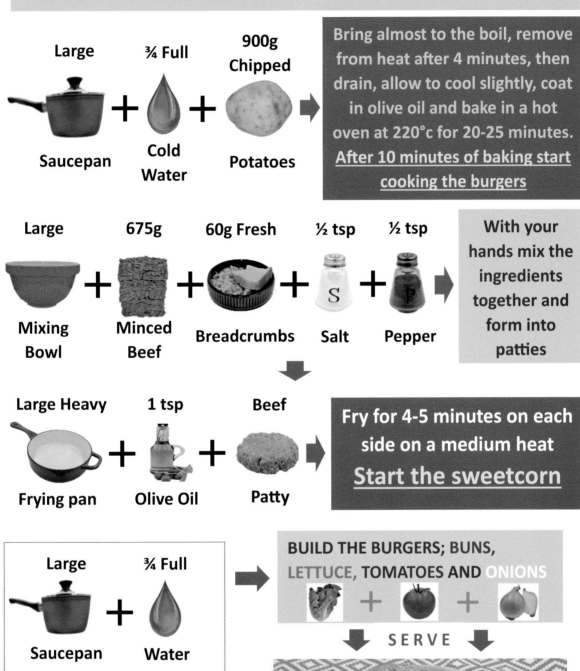

Large + ¾ Full + 900g Chipped

Saucepan + Cold Water + Potatoes

Bring almost to the boil, remove from heat after 4 minutes, then drain, allow to cool slightly, coat in olive oil and bake in a hot oven at 220°c for 20-25 minutes. After 10 minutes of baking start cooking the burgers

Large + 675g + 60g Fresh + ½ tsp + ½ tsp

Mixing Bowl + Minced Beef + Breadcrumbs + Salt + Pepper

With your hands mix the ingredients together and form into patties

Large Heavy + 1 tsp + Beef

Frying pan + Olive Oil + Patty

Fry for 4-5 minutes on each side on a medium heat
Start the sweetcorn

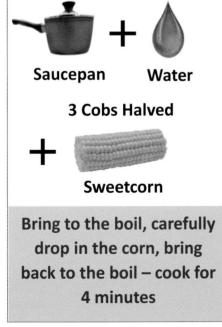

Large + ¾ Full

Saucepan + Water

3 Cobs Halved

+ Sweetcorn

Bring to the boil, carefully drop in the corn, bring back to the boil – cook for 4 minutes

BUILD THE BURGERS; BUNS, LETTUCE, TOMATOES AND ONIONS

+ +

SERVE

Roast Dinner

Ingredients

2 kg Whole Chicken

1 Teaspoon Olive Oil

¼ Teaspoon Salt

¼ Teaspoon Black Pepper

Water for Potatoes

1.2 kg Potatoes

2 Tablespoons Olive Oil

Water for Carrots

450 grams Carrots

¼ Teaspoon Salt

½ Teaspoon Sugar

Water for Peas

450 grams Peas

2 Tablespoons Plain Flour

500ml Chicken Stock

¼ Teaspoon Salt

¼ Teaspoon White Pepper

NOTES;

Any type of meat can be cooked in the same way; cooking with a casserole pot keeps your oven clean.

Maris Piper or King Edward potatoes are best for roasting.

Corn flour can replace plain flour if you like.

Pierce the skin of the chicken between the body and leg; if the juices run clear the chicken is cooked.

Cook chicken at 45 minutes per kilo plus 20 minutes.

Season the chicken to your liking.

Roast Dinner

I love a roast dinner, can be made with any meat or
plant-based alternative.   Set oven at 200°c   Serves 6

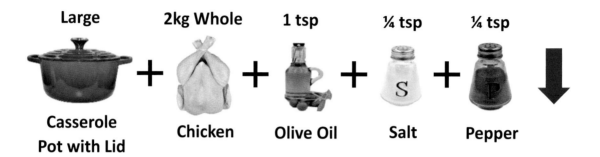

Large	2kg Whole	1 tsp	¼ tsp	¼ tsp
Casserole Pot with Lid	Chicken	Olive Oil	Salt	Pepper

Rub chicken with oil, season with salt & pepper and roast in the oven at 200°c for 1 hour 20 minutes with the lid on, then remove the lid and cook for a further 30 minutes, basting occasionally. Rest for 10 minutes. RETAIN THE JUICES **FROM THE CHICKEN FOR MAKING THE GRAVY.** USE THE SAME POT FOR MAKING THE GRAVY

WHILST CHICKEN IS COOKING START POTATOES

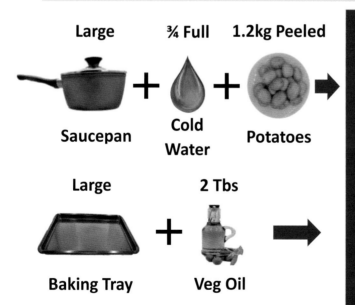

Large	¾ Full	1.2kg Peeled
Saucepan	Cold Water	Potatoes

Large	2 Tbs
Baking Tray	Veg Oil

Bring to the boil, simmer for 8 minutes, drain SET ASIDE. __At the point you remove the lid off the chicken__ put the baking tray with oil in the oven to heat, after 2 minutes add the SET-ASIDE potatoes to the tray and roast for the remaining 30 minutes

Start your vegetables while the chicken is resting

Medium	¾ Full	450g Sliced	¼ tsp	½ tsp	
Saucepan	+ Water	+ Carrots	+ Salt	+ Sugar	→ Bring to boil, simmer for 8 minutes, drain and **SERVE**

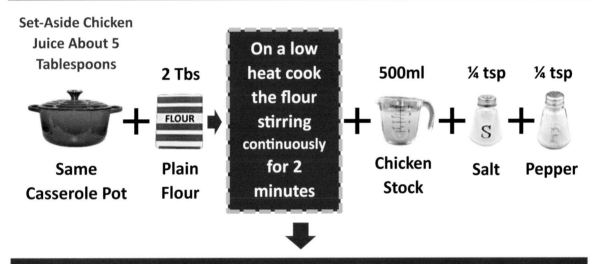

Medium	¾ Full	450g	
Saucepan	+ Water	+ Peas	→ Bring to the boil simmer for 5 minutes SERVE

WHILST VEGETABLES ARE COOKING START THE GRAVY

Set-Aside Chicken Juice About 5 Tablespoons	2 Tbs	On a low heat cook the flour stirring continuously for 2 minutes	500ml	¼ tsp	¼ tsp
Same Casserole Pot	+ Plain Flour	→	+ Chicken Stock	+ Salt	+ Pepper

Bring to the boil, reduce heat and simmer for 3 minutes stir regularly

CARVE THE CHICKEN, REMOVE ROASTED POTATOES FROM THE OVEN AND SERVE WITH THE VEGETABLES AND GRAVY →

Creamy Vegetable Curry
Ingredients

1 Tablespoon Vegetable Oil	1 Tablespoon Vegetable Oil
1 Small Onion	1 Large Onion
2 Cloves Garlic	2 Cloves Garlic
15 grams Fresh Ginger	1 Courgette
2 Teaspoons Tomato Puree	1 Green Pepper
6 Large Tomatoes	150 grams French Beans
4 Whole Cardamom Pods	1 Large Carrot
1 Tablespoon Medium Curry Powder	150 grams Plain Yogurt
150ml Water	150 grams Spinach
1 Teaspoon Salt	15 grams Fresh Coriander
½ Teaspoon Black Pepper	
350 grams Basmati Rice	
700ml Water	

NOTES;

For vegan option, plain soya yogurt can replace the dairy yogurt.

Use the main vegetables of your choice.

Creamy Vegetable Curry

A treat for the tastebuds, any vegetable can be used; whatever is in your fridge.   Serves 6

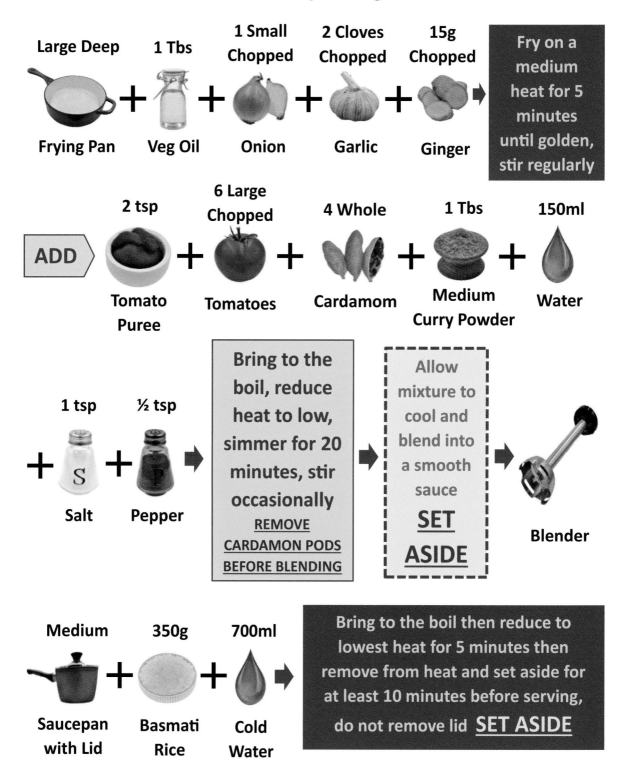

Large Deep + **1 Tbs** + **1 Small Chopped** + **2 Cloves Chopped** + **15g Chopped** → Fry on a medium heat for 5 minutes until golden, stir regularly

Frying Pan   Veg Oil   Onion   Garlic   Ginger

ADD > **2 tsp** Tomato Puree + **6 Large Chopped** Tomatoes + **4 Whole** Cardamom + **1 Tbs** Medium Curry Powder + **150ml** Water

+ **1 tsp** Salt + **½ tsp** Pepper → Bring to the boil, reduce heat to low, simmer for 20 minutes, stir occasionally REMOVE CARDAMON PODS BEFORE BLENDING → Allow mixture to cool and blend into a smooth sauce SET ASIDE → Blender

Medium Saucepan with Lid + **350g** Basmati Rice + **700ml** Cold Water → Bring to the boil then reduce to lowest heat for 5 minutes then remove from heat and set aside for at least 10 minutes before serving, do not remove lid SET ASIDE

27

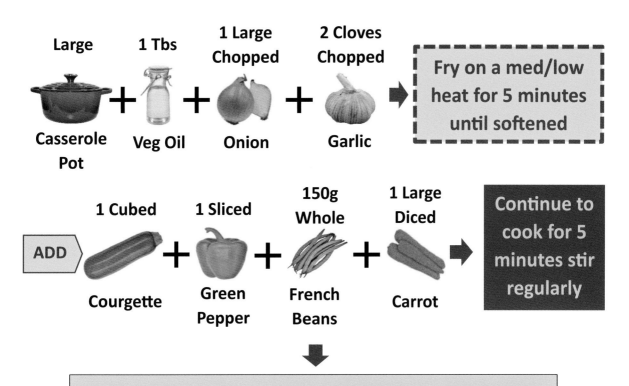

Large + 1 Tbs + 1 Large Chopped + 2 Cloves Chopped

Casserole Pot | Veg Oil | Onion | Garlic

Fry on a med/low heat for 5 minutes until softened

ADD 1 Cubed + 1 Sliced + 150g Whole + 1 Large Diced

Courgette | Green Pepper | French Beans | Carrot

Continue to cook for 5 minutes stir regularly

ADD THE SET-ASIDE TOMATO MIXTURE
COVER AND COOK FOR A FURTHER 10 MINUTES ON A LOW/MED HEAT

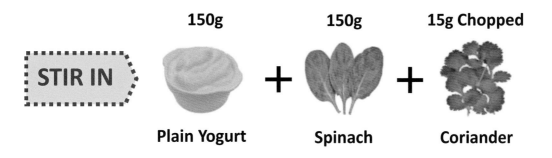

STIR IN 150g + 150g + 15g Chopped

Plain Yogurt | Spinach | Coriander

COOK FOR 1 MORE MINUTE AND SERVE WITH RICE

Macaroni Cheese

Ingredients

500 grams Macaroni

Water for Macaroni

½ Teaspoon Salt

50 grams Butter

1 Tablespoon Olive Oil

5 Tablespoons Plain Flour

900ml Whole Milk

½ Teaspoon Salt

¼ Teaspoon Black Pepper

1 Teaspoon Dijon Mustard

125 grams Medium Cheddar

125 grams Mature Cheddar

200 grams Medium Cheddar

25 grams Fresh Breadcrumbs

NOTES;

Fry some sliced leeks as the first step for a twist on this classic dish.

For a vegan alternative replace dairy ingredients with plant-based cheese and butter as well as 50% soya 50% oat milk.

Macaroni Cheese

A British classic with many variations, a favourite with the Victorians.   Set oven at 200°c.   Serves 6

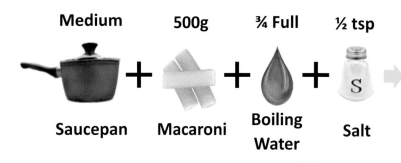

| Medium | 500g | ¾ Full | ½ tsp | Bring back to the boil, reduce heat to low, and simmer for 7 minutes then drain well |
| Saucepan | Macaroni | Boiling Water | Salt | |

WHILST MACARONI IS COOKING, START THE SAUCE

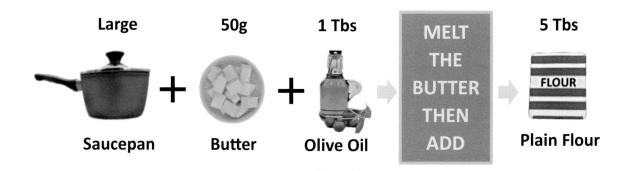

| Large | 50g | 1 Tbs | MELT THE BUTTER THEN ADD | 5 Tbs |
| Saucepan | Butter | Olive Oil | | Plain Flour |

STIR CONSTANTLY ON A LOW HEAT FOR 2 MINUTES

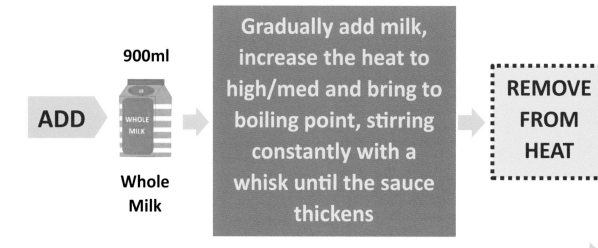

ADD

900ml

Whole Milk

Gradually add milk, increase the heat to high/med and bring to boiling point, stirring constantly with a whisk until the sauce thickens

REMOVE FROM HEAT

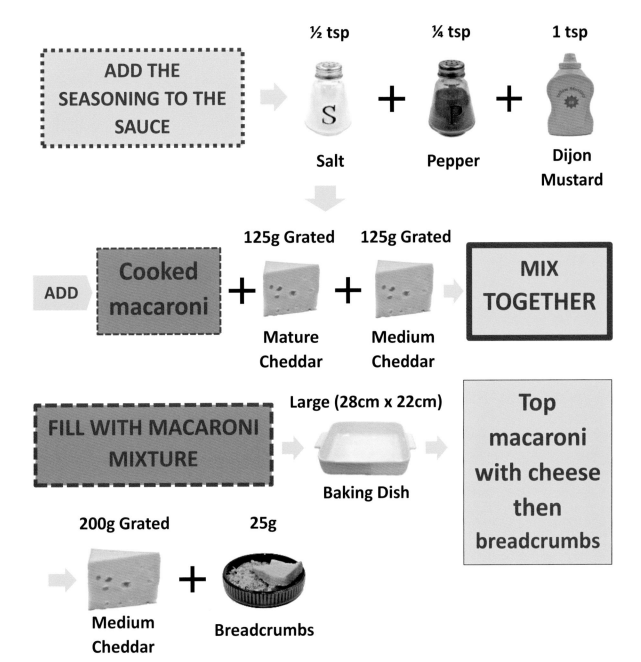

ADD THE SEASONING TO THE SAUCE

½ tsp — Salt

¼ tsp — Pepper

1 tsp — Dijon Mustard

ADD — Cooked macaroni + 125g Grated Mature Cheddar + 125g Grated Medium Cheddar → MIX TOGETHER

FILL WITH MACARONI MIXTURE → Large (28cm x 22cm) Baking Dish → Top macaroni with cheese then breadcrumbs

200g Grated Medium Cheddar + 25g Breadcrumbs

Bake for 15 minutes at 200°c

Chicken and Rice
Ingredients

2 Tablespoons Olive Oil

1kg Chicken Legs

1 Large Onion

160 grams Carrots

2 Cloves Garlic

2 Sticks of Celery

110 grams French Beans

120 grams Leeks

300 grams Basmati Rice

1 Teaspoon Salt

½ Teaspoon Black Pepper

750ml Chicken Stock

NOTES;

When covering the pan with foil be careful as the pan will be hot- use oven gloves.

You can use arborio rice.

For vegan option replace chicken stock with vegetable and use large, whole mushrooms instead of chicken.

29

Chicken and Rice

Really easy and really tasty, my children love this dish.

Serves 6

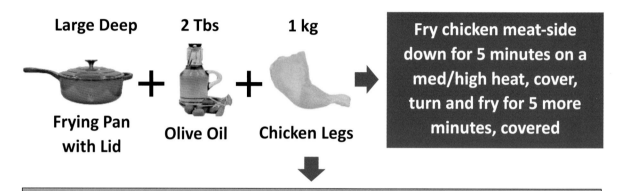

Large Deep + **2 Tbs** + **1 kg** → Fry chicken meat-side down for 5 minutes on a med/high heat, cover, turn and fry for 5 more minutes, covered

Frying Pan with Lid   **Olive Oil**   **Chicken Legs**

DRAIN OFF JUICES AND RETAIN   SET CHICKEN ASIDE

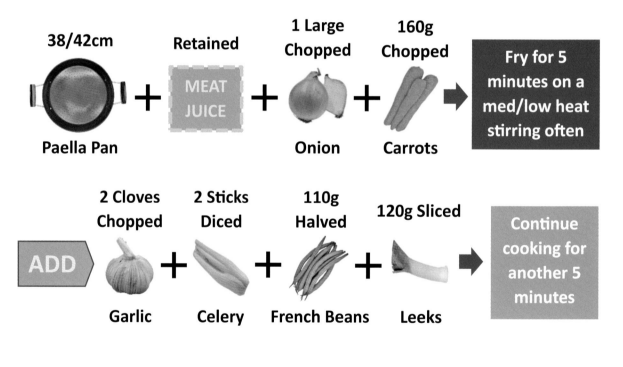

38/42cm + **Retained** + **1 Large Chopped** + **160g Chopped** → Fry for 5 minutes on a med/low heat stirring often

Paella Pan   MEAT JUICE   **Onion**   **Carrots**

ADD **2 Cloves Chopped** + **2 Sticks Diced** + **110g Halved** + **120g Sliced** → Continue cooking for another 5 minutes

Garlic   **Celery**   **French Beans**   **Leeks**

ADD **300g** → STIR THE RICE IN → **1 tsp** + **½ tsp** + **750ml**

Basmati Rice   **Salt**   **Pepper**   **Chicken Stock**

ADD → SET-ASIDE CHICKEN → **Nestle the chicken legs into the mixture so that they are half buried**

COVER THE PAN WITH FOIL

COOK ON A LOW HEAT FOR 20 MINUTES

SERVE

Shepherd's Pie

Ingredients

1 Tablespoon Olive Oil

2 Medium Onions

2 Cloves Garlic

2 Large Carrots

1 Stick of Celery

1 Tablespoon Olive Oil

650 grams Minced Lamb

1 Tablespoon Tomato Puree

1 Teaspoon Mixed Herbs

½ Teaspoon Salt

½ Teaspoon Black Pepper

¼ Teaspoon Ground Cinnamon

2 Tablespoons Plain Flour

450ml Vegetable Stock

Water for Potatoes

1.3kg Potatoes

Knob of Butter (10 grams)

2 Tablespoons Milk

1 Teaspoon Salt

1 Tomato

Drizzle of Olive Oil

NOTES;

A floury or waxy potato like Desiree is best for mashing.

For a vegan alternative replace the dairy with plant-based alternatives and replace the meat with a 50/50 mix of puy lentils and split red lentils.

For a cottage pie replace the lamb with Beef.

Shepherd's Pie

Everyone's favourite, proper comfort food
Set the oven to 220°c   Serves 6

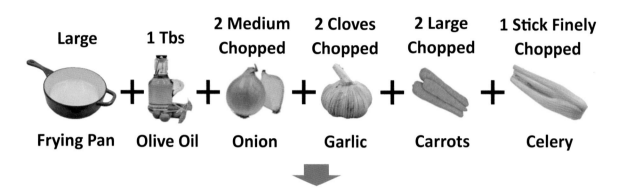

Large	1 Tbs	2 Medium Chopped	2 Cloves Chopped	2 Large Chopped	1 Stick Finely Chopped
Frying Pan	Olive Oil	Onion	Garlic	Carrots	Celery

FRY ON MEDIUM HEAT FOR 5 MINUTES, STIR REGULARLY

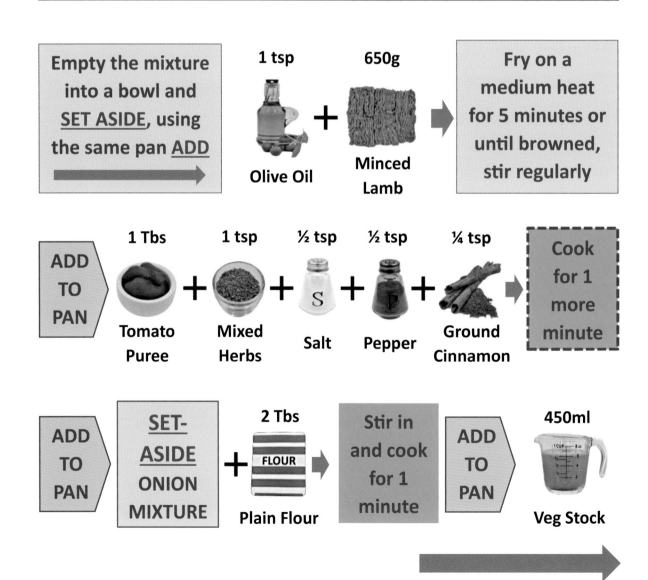

Empty the mixture into a bowl and SET ASIDE, using the same pan ADD

1 tsp Olive Oil + 650g Minced Lamb

Fry on a medium heat for 5 minutes or until browned, stir regularly

ADD TO PAN

1 Tbs Tomato Puree + 1 tsp Mixed Herbs + ½ tsp Salt + ½ tsp Pepper + ¼ tsp Ground Cinnamon

Cook for 1 more minute

ADD TO PAN

SET-ASIDE ONION MIXTURE + 2 Tbs Plain Flour

Stir in and cook for 1 minute

ADD TO PAN

450ml Veg Stock

COOK FOR 10 MINUTES ON A LOW HEAT, THEN EMPTY INTO A BAKING DISH AND ALLOW TO COOL

WHILST THE MEAT IS COOKING AND COOLING, START THE MASH POTATO TOPPING

Large | ¾ Full | 1.3kg Peeled and Halved

Saucepan + Water + Potatoes

Bring to the boil, reduce heat, simmer for 10 minutes then remove from heat. After another 10 minutes drain and mash with a knob of butter

+ 2 Tbs Milk + 1 tsp Salt

TOP THE MEAT WITH THE MASH POTATOES

LIGHTLY RUN A FORK OVER THE MASH TO ROUGHEN

PLACE ON TOP SLICES OF TOMATO

AND A DRIZZLE OF OLIVE OIL

Bake in hot oven at 220°c for 20 minutes

SERVE WITH A VEGETABLE OF YOUR CHOICE

Lamb Tagine

Ingredients

1 Teaspoon Olive Oil

500 grams Diced Leg of Lamb

1 Tablespoon Olive Oil

1 Large Onion

4 Cloves Garlic

5 Tablespoons Water

½ Teaspoon Ground Turmeric

½ Teaspoon Ground Ginger

1 Teaspoon Ground Cumin

½ Teaspoon Black Pepper

½ Teaspoon Ground Coriander

¼ Teaspoon Mild Chilli Powder

½ Teaspoon Sweet Paprika

½ Teaspoon Ground Cinnamon

½ Teaspoon Garam Masala

¼ Teaspoon Ground Nutmeg

2 Teaspoons Tomato Puree

4 Large Tomatoes

500ml Vegetable Stock

1 Teaspoon Salt

100 grams Aubergine

100g grams Courgette

80 grams French Beans

1 Green Pepper

200 grams Carrots

400 grams Chickpeas (1 Tin)

1 Lemon

90 grams Dried Apricots

120 grams Dried Prunes

60 grams Sultanas

20 grams Fresh Coriander

450ml Boiling Water

350 grams Couscous

NOTES;

A traditional Tagine can be used.

Drain chickpeas.

Leave out the meat and replace with butternut squash for a vegan alternative.

Use whatever vegetables you desire.

Lamb Tagine

A Middle Eastern dish, full of flavour.
Set oven to 180°c   Serves 6

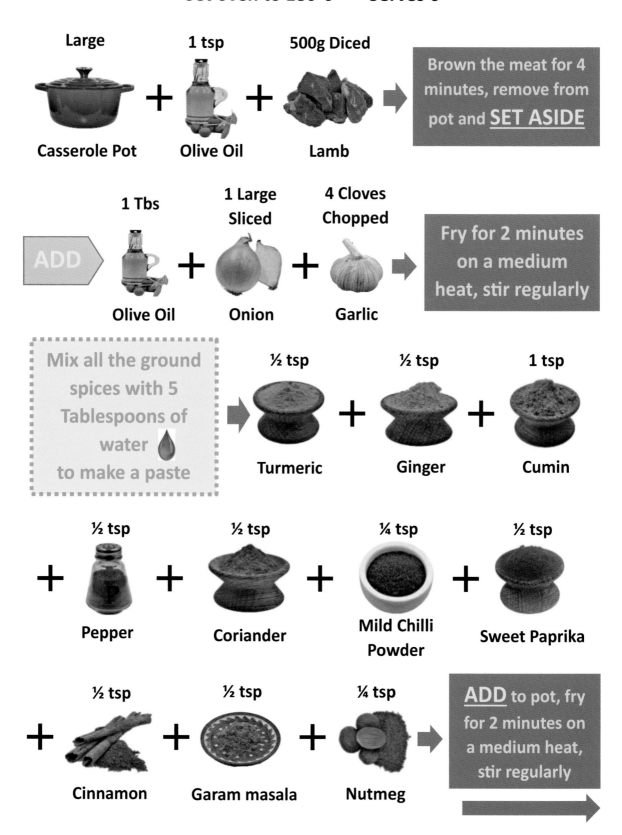

Large
Casserole Pot

1 tsp
Olive Oil

500g Diced
Lamb

Brown the meat for 4 minutes, remove from pot and **SET ASIDE**

ADD

1 Tbs
Olive Oil

1 Large Sliced
Onion

4 Cloves Chopped
Garlic

Fry for 2 minutes on a medium heat, stir regularly

Mix all the ground spices with 5 Tablespoons of water to make a paste

½ tsp
Turmeric

½ tsp
Ginger

1 tsp
Cumin

½ tsp
Pepper

½ tsp
Coriander

¼ tsp
Mild Chilli Powder

½ tsp
Sweet Paprika

½ tsp
Cinnamon

½ tsp
Garam masala

¼ tsp
Nutmeg

ADD to pot, fry for 2 minutes on a medium heat, stir regularly

ADD 2 tsp **Tomato Puree** → Fry for 1 minute stirring constantly → **ADD** 4 Large Quartered **Tomatoes** + 500ml **Veg Stock**

+ **SET-ASIDE LAMB** + 1 tsp **Salt** + 100g Cubed **Aubergine** + 100g Cubed **Courgette** + 80g Halved **French Bean**

+ 1 Sliced **Green Pepper** + 200g Cubed **Carrots** + 240g (1 Tin) **Chickpeas** + 1 Halved **Lemon** → Bake in the oven with the lid on for 1 hour at 180°c, stir occasionally

ADD 90g **Apricots** + 120g **Prunes** + 60g **Sultanas** → Cook for a further 30 minutes then mix in → 20g Chopped **Fresh Coriander**

Large **Heat-Proof Bowl** + 450ml **Boiling Water** + 350g **Couscous**

ADD the boiling water, leave to stand for 5 minutes then fork through. **SERVE WITH THE LAMB TAGINE** →

31

Fish, Chips and Mushy Peas

Ingredients

Water for Potatoes

900 grams Potatoes

6 Tablespoons Plain Flour

3 Tablespoons Corn Flour

2 Teaspoons Bicarbonate of Soda

½ Teaspoon Salt

¼ Teaspoon Black Pepper

1 Teaspoon Oregano

130ml Cold Water

1 Teaspoon Garlic Granules

3 Tablespoons Plain Flour

½ Teaspoon Salt

¼ Teaspoon Black Pepper

1 Litre Vegetable Oil

460 grams Cod Fillet

2 Tins of Marrowfat Peas (600g total)

4 Large Mint Leaves

¼ Teaspoon Lemon Juice

Pinch of Salt

NOTES;

Chips should be about the size of an adult finger.

Use soda water or beer to replace bi-carb and water.

When placing the fish in the hot oil turn off the heat, gently lower the fish in the oil in a motion away from yourself, keep the handle of the pan to the back of the stove to avoid any accidents, turn back on the heat once fish is in the oil.

Cook fish in batches, keep warm in the oven.

You can use garden peas for the mushy peas: finely chop some garlic and a few mint leaves add to the water, drain, then add salt, knob of butter and a squeeze of lemon. Mash.

For vegan option replace fish with carrot batons, broccoli spears and sweet potato batons or Tofu batons.

Fish, Chips and Mushy Peas

A British dish, light and delicious.

Set oven to 220°c   Serves 5

Large

Enough to Cover

900g Peeled, Chipped

Bring almost to the boil, remove from heat after 4 minutes, drain, allow to cool slightly, coat in olive oil and bake in a hot oven at 220°c for 20-25 minutes.

Saucepan   Cold Water   Potatoes

MAKE THE BATTER

Large   6 Tbs   3 Tbs   2 tsp   ½ tsp   ¼ tsp

Bowl   Plain Flour   Corn Flour   Bicarbonate of Soda   Salt   Pepper

1 tsp   130ml   1 tsp

Oregano   Cold Water   Garlic Granules

Mix the ingredients into a smooth batter about the consistency of single cream **SET ASIDE**

Remove the skin from the Cod Fillet

Remove the skin by placing the fish on a flat surface skin-side down. With a large, sharp knife cut in between the meat and skin- as close to the skin as possible. Keeping your knife flat to the surface, apply slight downward pressure and pull the knife through the length of the fillet. **SET ASIDE**

Large	3 Tbs	½ tsp	¼ tsp	

| Plate | Plain Flour | Salt | Pepper | **DUST THE FISH IN FLOUR** |

Large Deep | 1 Litre

Heavy Pan | Veg Oil

Heat the oil to 180°c Drop a bit of the batter in the oil it should sizzle and float to the surface immediately

Dip the dusted fish in the SET-ASIDE batter, carefully place the fish in the hot oil using tongs

460g Cut into 3-inch Pieces

Cod Fillet

Cook each piece for 3 minutes then turn and cook for a further 3 minutes

Remove with a slotted spoon and drain on a rack with some kitchen paper under the rack

Small	2 Tins (600g)	4 leaves Chopped	¼ tsp Juice	Pinch

| Saucepan | Marrowfat Peas | Fresh Mint | Lemon | Salt |

Heat the peas and mint to near boiling point, reduce heat to low, cook for 3 minutes MASH PEAS LIGHTLY SERVE with the FISH AND CHIPS →

Roasted Red Pepper Pasta

Ingredients

2 Tablespoons Olive Oil

4 Red Peppers

1 Large Onion

1 Large Carrot

1 Tablespoon Olive Oil

1 Large Onion

3 Cloves Garlic

3 Tablespoons Water

½ Teaspoon Sweet Paprika

1 Tablespoon Sugar

1 Tablespoon Tomato Puree

1 Teaspoon Salt

½ Teaspoon Black Pepper

350ml Chicken Stock

10 grams Fresh Basil

400 grams Tinned tomatoes

2 Green Peppers

140 grams French Beans

Juice of ½ a Lemon

Water For Pasta

500 grams Conchiglie

Cheese

NOTES;

Equally delicious served with sausages and mash.

Any browned meat can be added to the pot before cooking for 20 minutes or any type of pulse.

5 fresh tomatoes can be used instead of tinned.

Replace chicken stock with vegetable stock for vegan alternative.

Roasted Red Pepper Pasta

This delicious sauce can easily be served with
sausages and mash.   Set oven to 220°c

Serves 5

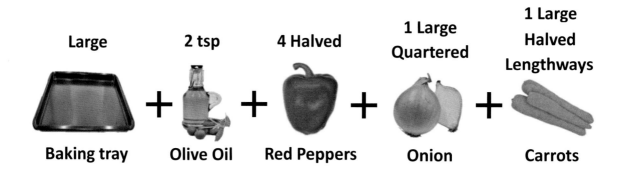

Large	2 tsp	4 Halved	1 Large Quartered	1 Large Halved Lengthways
Baking tray	Olive Oil	Red Peppers	Onion	Carrots

Coat the peppers, onion and carrot in oil, roast for 25 minutes SET ASIDE

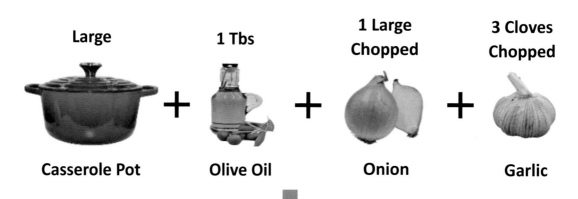

Large	1 Tbs	1 Large Chopped	3 Cloves Chopped
Casserole Pot	Olive Oil	Onion	Garlic

Fry on a med/high heat for 4 minutes stirring continually

ADD

3 Tbs	½ tsp	1 Tbs
Water	Sweet Paprika	Sugar

Cook for 2 minutes stirring continually

ADD

1 Tbs
Tomato Puree
+
1 tsp
Salt
+
½ tsp
Pepper
→
Cook for 1 more minute

Blender
+
SET ASIDE pepper, onion and carrot
+
350ml Chicken Stock
+
10g Fresh Basil
→
Blend until smooth then add to the pot

ADD

400g Tinned Tomatoes
+
2 Finely Chopped Green Pepper
+
140g Halved French Beans
+
Juice of ½ Lemon
→
Cook for 20 minutes with the lid on, stir occasionally

Large Saucepan
+
¾ Full Water
+
500g Conchiglie
→
Bring water to the boil, add Conchiglie, cook on a medium heat for 10-11 minutes, drain and <u>mix immediately with sauce</u>.

SERVE WITH A GRATED CHEESE OF YOUR CHOICE
→
Cheese
→

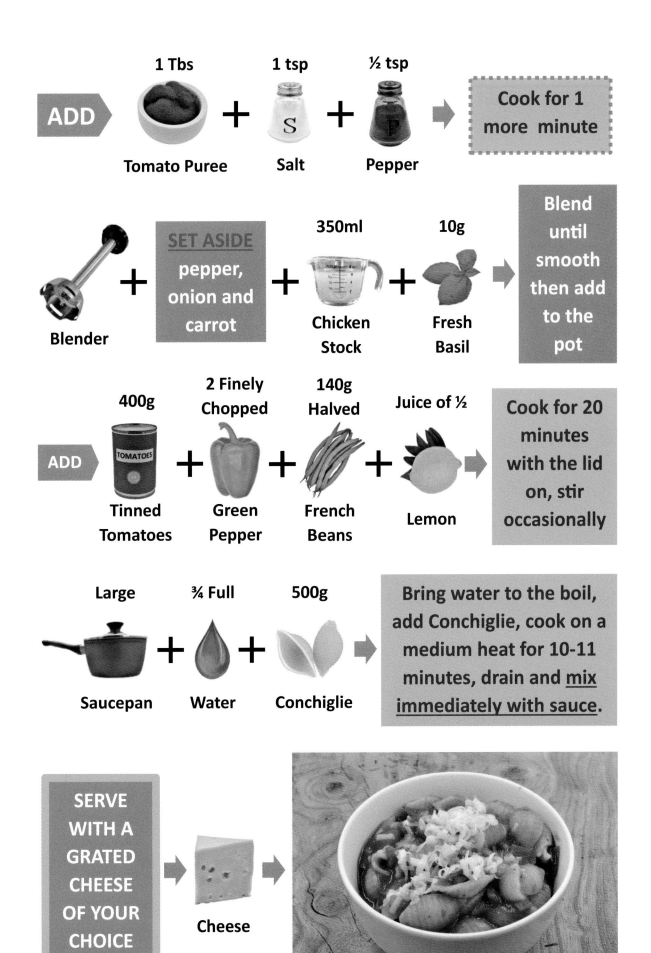

Chilli Con Carne

Ingredients

1 Tablespoon Olive Oil

500g Minced Beef

1 Large Onion

4 Cloves Garlic

3 Fresh Green Chilli Peppers

1 Red Pepper

1 Teaspoon Sweet Paprika

½ Teaspoon Ground Cumin

½ Teaspoon Chilli Powder

1 Tablespoon Tomato Puree

400 grams Tinned Tomatoes

300ml Beef Stock

1 Tablespoon Corn Flour

1 Teaspoon Salt

½ Teaspoon Black Pepper

2 Teaspoons Sugar

1 Teaspoon Lemon Juice

400 grams Kidney Beans

Water for Rice

350 grams Long Grain Rice

NOTES;

Make the chilli hotter by finely chopping the green chillies.

Use tinned kidney beans.

For a vegan alternative use 50% green lentils and 50% puy lentils to replace the meat and replace beef stock with vegetable stock, add the lentils at the point you add the stock, rinse the lentils well.

Chilli Con Carne

This delicious dish can be as hot or as mild as you like.

Serves 5

Large   **1 tsp**   **500g Minced**

Frying Pan with Lid   Olive Oil   Beef

Brown the mince for 3 minutes on a high heat stirring regularly

ADD

1 Large Chopped   **4 Cloves Chopped**   **3 Whole**   **1 Finely Chopped**

Onion   Garlic   Fresh Green Chillies   Red Pepper

Reduce heat to medium, cook for 3 minutes stirring regularly

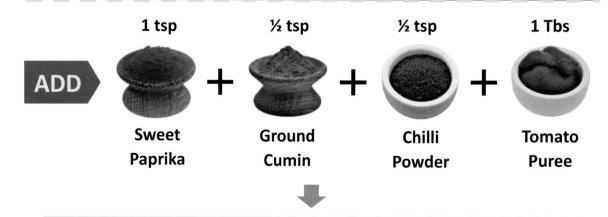

ADD

1 tsp   **½ tsp**   **½ tsp**   **1 Tbs**

Sweet Paprika   Ground Cumin   Chilli Powder   Tomato Puree

Cook for 1 minute stirring continually

ADD

400g Chopped	300ml	1 Tbs	1 tsp	½ tsp
Tinned Tomatoes	Beef Stock	Corn Flour	Salt	Pepper

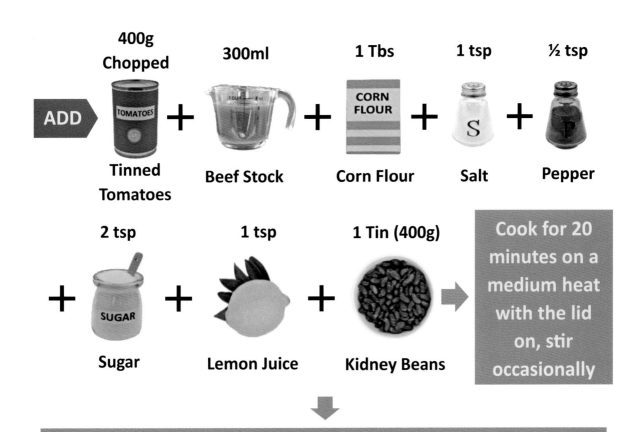

2 tsp	1 tsp	1 Tin (400g)
Sugar	Lemon Juice	Kidney Beans

Cook for 20 minutes on a medium heat with the lid on, stir occasionally

While the chilli is cooking start your rice

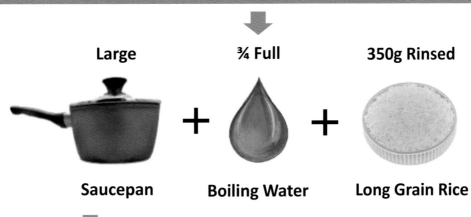

Large	¾ Full	350g Rinsed
Saucepan	Boiling Water	Long Grain Rice

Bring water to the boil, add rice and bring back to the boil, stir and simmer uncovered on a low heat for 10/12 minutes, DRAIN AND SERVE WITH THE CHILLI

YOUR NOTES

Salmon, Pea and Asparagus Risotto
Ingredients

Water for Poaching Fish

500 grams Fresh Salmon Fillet (skinless)

1 Whole Bay leaf

1 Tablespoon Vegetable Oil

35 grams Butter

1 Small Onion

350 grams Arborio Rice

100ml White Wine

350ml Vegetable Stock

1 Teaspoon Salt

¼ Teaspoon Black pepper

Water for Peas and Asparagus

100 grams Asparagus

200 grams Peas

100ml Single Cream

15 grams Parsley

1 Lemon

NOTES;

For a vegan option replace fish with butternut squash, don't part boil. Use plant-based butter and cream.

Leave out the wine for a slightly different flavour.

Make sure all the water is drained out of the saucepan with the poached salmon, before shaking to flake the fish.

Salmon, Pea and Asparagus Risotto

A delicious Risotto.   **Serves 6**

Medium	Enough to Cover	500g Fresh Fillet	1 Whole
Saucepan with Lid	Water	Fresh Salmon (skinless)	Bay Leaf

Bring to a boil, cover and reduce heat to lowest for 8 minutes, drain and keeping the fish in the saucepan SET ASIDE

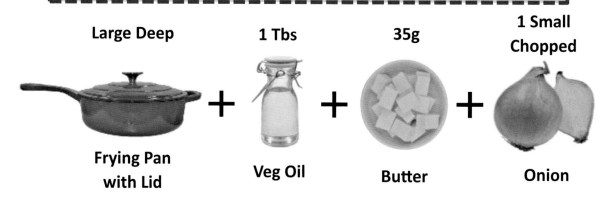

Large Deep	1 Tbs	35g	1 Small Chopped
Frying Pan with Lid	Veg Oil	Butter	Onion

Cook on med/low heat for 4 minutes stir regularly

THEN ADD

350g

Arborio Rice

Cook on med/low heat for 1 minute stir regularly

THEN ADD

100ml

White Wine

→

When the wine has been absorbed

ADD

350ml

Veg Stock

+ **1 tsp** Salt + **¼ tsp** Pepper →

Cover and cook on med/low heat for 15 minutes, stir occasionally

---

Small Saucepan + **¾ Full** Water + **100g Chopped into Quarters** Asparagus + **200g** Peas

↓

After 10 minutes cook the peas and asparagus in boiling water for 2 minutes, then DRAIN

100ml Cream + **15g Chopped** Parsley + **1 Quartered** Lemon

Shake the SET-ASIDE FISH in the saucepan keeping the lid on, to flake

Mix into the rice the fish, peas and asparagus, stir in the single cream and parsley. Serve with a quartered lemon

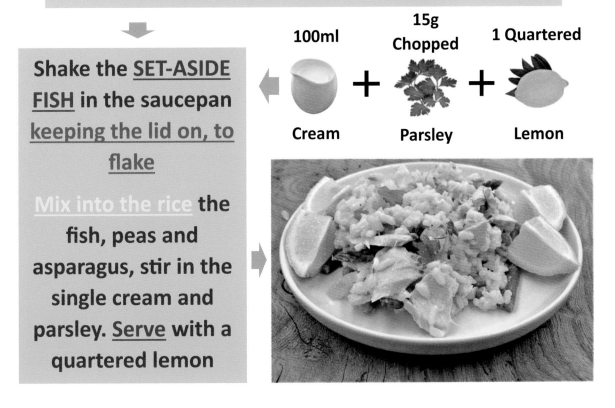

Courgette Soup
Ingredients

1 Tablespoon Vegetable Oil

20 grams Fresh Ginger

4 Whole Cardamom Pods

1 kg Courgettes

200ml Vegetable Stock

800ml Water

90 grams Rice

90 grams Red Lentils

1 Teaspoon Salt

¼ Teaspoon Black Pepper

Water for Pasta

400 grams Fusilli Pasta

NOTES;

Any pasta can be used.

Any rice can be used.

Courgette Soup

This recipe came about because of a glut of courgettes one summer, this is my children's favourite dish, serve with or without pasta.   Serves 6

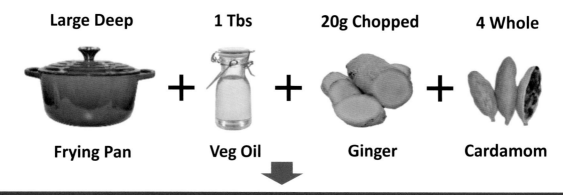

Large Deep	1 Tbs	20g Chopped	4 Whole
Frying Pan	Veg Oil	Ginger	Cardamom

Cook on med/low heat for 1 minute, stir regularly

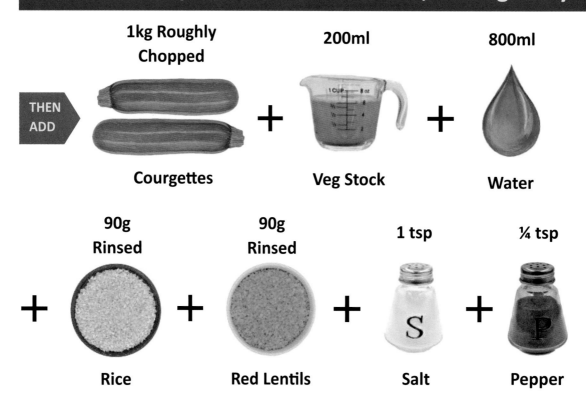

THEN ADD

1kg Roughly Chopped	200ml	800ml
Courgettes	Veg Stock	Water

90g Rinsed	90g Rinsed	1 tsp	¼ tsp
Rice	Red Lentils	Salt	Pepper

Bring to the boil, reduce heat to low, cover and simmer for 20 minutes. The cardamom pods should float to the surface- pick them out, squeeze the seeds into the pot and discard the pod.

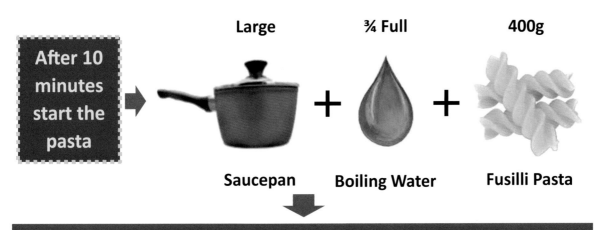

After 10 minutes start the pasta

Large
Saucepan

¾ Full
Boiling Water

400g
Fusilli Pasta

Bring back to the boil, reduce heat to low and simmer for 8-10 minutes

Cooked Courgettes

Stick Blender

BLEND COURGETTES UNTIL SMOOTH

Drain pasta and mix with your courgette soup SERVE

Without Pasta

With Pasta

Tofu Pad Thai

Ingredients

Water for Noodles

500 grams Medium Rice Noodles

Water for Tamarind

40 grams Wet Tamarind

1 Tablespoon Fish Sauce

1 Tablespoon Palm Sugar

1 Teaspoon Dark Soy

1 Teaspoon Hot Chilli Sauce

1 Tablespoon Sweet Chilli Sauce

1 Tablespoon Vegetable Oil

260 grams Firm Tofu

1 Tablespoon Vegetable Oil

150 grams Shallots

4 Cloves Garlic

2 Large Eggs

200 grams Bean Sprouts

1 Large Carrot

100 grams Spring Onions
(1 Bunch)

80 grams Roasted Peanuts

30 grams Roasted Peanuts

2 Limes

NOTES;

For vegan option omit the fish sauce and egg.

Tamarind paste can be used, mixed with a little water.

For those with a peanut allergy, replace with toasted cashew nuts.

When making the fish sauce mixture gently heat until the sugar has dissolved; the mixture should be smooth and silky between your fingers.

Tofu Pad Thai

This delicious Pad Thai can be made with chicken, prawns, beef or pork.   Serves 5

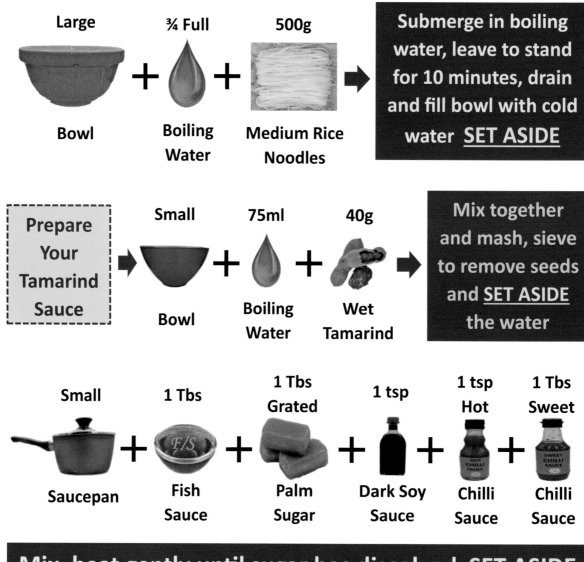

Large + **¾ Full** + **500g** → Submerge in boiling water, leave to stand for 10 minutes, drain and fill bowl with cold water **SET ASIDE**

Bowl   Boiling Water   Medium Rice Noodles

Prepare Your Tamarind Sauce → **Small** + **75ml** + **40g** → Mix together and mash, sieve to remove seeds and **SET ASIDE** the water

Bowl   Boiling Water   Wet Tamarind

Small + **1 Tbs** + **1 Tbs Grated** + **1 tsp** + **1 tsp Hot** + **1 Tbs Sweet**

Saucepan   Fish Sauce   Palm Sugar   Dark Soy Sauce   Chilli Sauce   Chilli Sauce

Mix, heat gently until sugar has dissolved SET ASIDE

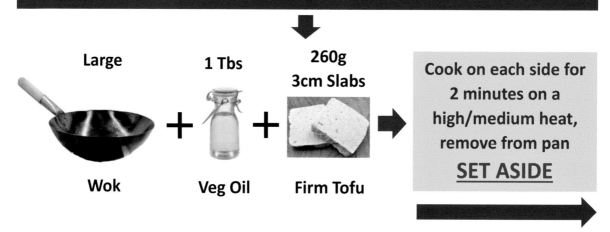

Large + **1 Tbs** + **260g 3cm Slabs** → Cook on each side for 2 minutes on a high/medium heat, remove from pan **SET ASIDE**

Wok   Veg Oil   Firm Tofu

37

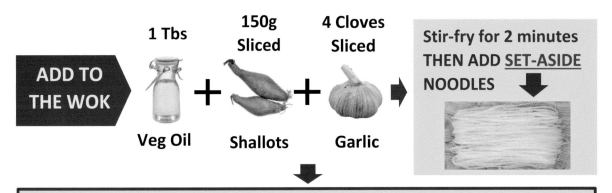

ADD TO THE WOK

1 Tbs
Veg Oil

+

150g
Sliced
Shallots

+

4 Cloves
Sliced
Garlic

→

Stir-fry for 2 minutes THEN ADD <u>SET-ASIDE</u> NOODLES ↓

Cook the noodles for 1 minute on a high heat stirring continually

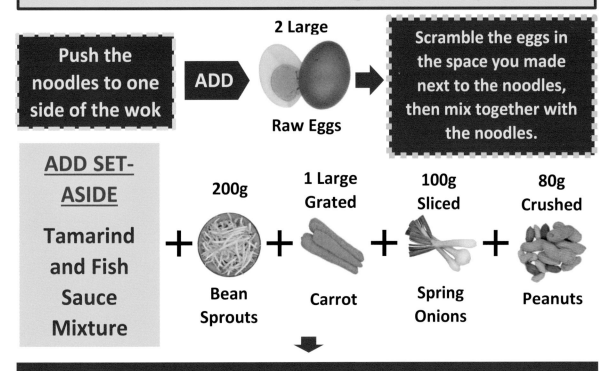

Push the noodles to one side of the wok

ADD

2 Large
Raw Eggs

→

Scramble the eggs in the space you made next to the noodles, then mix together with the noodles.

ADD SET-ASIDE

Tamarind and Fish Sauce Mixture

+

200g
Bean Sprouts

+

1 Large
Grated
Carrot

+

100g
Sliced
Spring Onions

+

80g
Crushed
Peanuts

STIR REGULARLY FOR 3 MINUTES ON A HIGH HEAT

ADD A LITTLE WATER OR VEGETABLE STOCK IF TOO DRY

SPRINKLE OVER ROASTED PEANUTS

30g Crushed

SERVE WITH QUARTERED LIMES

2   Limes

Chicken Biriyani

Ingredients

500 grams Diced Chicken Breast

150 grams Plain Yogurt

1 Tablespoon Vegetable Oil

4 Cloves Garlic

1 Teaspoon Ground Coriander

1 Teaspoon Ground Cumin

½ Teaspoon Ground Ginger

1 Teaspoon Salt

½ Teaspoon Black Pepper

½ Teaspoon Mild Chilli Powder

½ Teaspoon Turmeric

½ Teaspoon Ground Fenugreek

½ Teaspoon Garlic Granules

½ Teaspoon Ground Nutmeg

1 Teaspoon Garam Masala

Juice of 1 Lemon

Rind of ½ a Lemon

2 Litres Boiling Water

400 grams Basmati Rice

2 Sticks Cinnamon

1 Teaspoon Salt

½ Teaspoon Black Pepper

4 Whole Cloves

4 Whole Cardamom

2 Whole Star Anise

1 Tablespoon Vegetable Oil

1 Small Onion

150ml Chicken Stock

1 Green Pepper

2 Tomatoes

60 grams Sultanas

300 grams Plain Yogurt

30 grams Fresh Coriander

NOTES;

You can steam the dish in the oven, place a layer of baking paper over the last layer of rice then put the lid on and bake at 180°c for 20-25 minutes.

For a vegan alternative leave out the meat and replace with butternut squash and courgettes- cut in squash ball size chunks- and change the stock to vegetable.

Chicken Biriyani

An Indian dish, full of flavour.   Serves 6

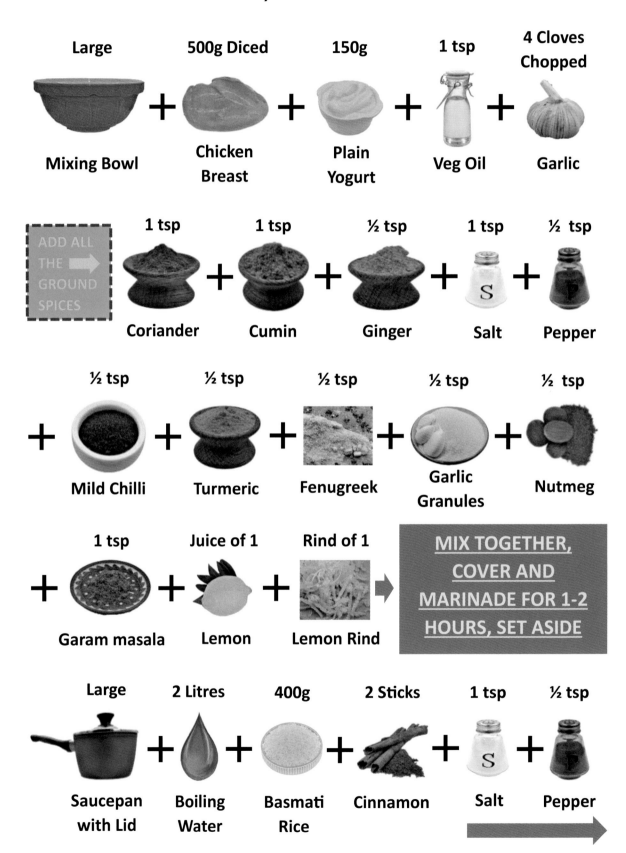

Large — Mixing Bowl

+

500g Diced — Chicken Breast

+

150g — Plain Yogurt

+

1 tsp — Veg Oil

+

4 Cloves Chopped — Garlic

ADD ALL THE GROUND SPICES

1 tsp — Coriander

+

1 tsp — Cumin

+

½ tsp — Ginger

+

1 tsp — Salt

+

½ tsp — Pepper

+

½ tsp — Mild Chilli

+

½ tsp — Turmeric

+

½ tsp — Fenugreek

+

½ tsp — Garlic Granules

+

½ tsp — Nutmeg

+

1 tsp — Garam masala

+

Juice of 1 — Lemon

+

Rind of 1 — Lemon Rind

MIX TOGETHER, COVER AND MARINADE FOR 1-2 HOURS, SET ASIDE

Large — Saucepan with Lid

+

2 Litres — Boiling Water

+

400g — Basmati Rice

+

2 Sticks — Cinnamon

+

1 tsp — Salt

+

½ tsp — Pepper

4 Whole + **4 Whole** + **2 Whole** → **PART-COOK THE RICE**
Bring back to boiling point, stir and simmer for 6 minutes, drain, then **SET ASIDE**

Cloves   Cardamom   Star Anise

Large Deep + **1 tsp** + **1 Small Chopped** → Fry for 2 minutes on a med/high heat, stir regularly

Frying Pan   Veg Oil   Onion

ADD ▸ **MARINATED CHICKEN MIXTURE** → Fry for 5 minutes on a med/high heat, stir regularly **ADD** ▸ **150ml** Chicken Stock

1 Sliced + **2 Chopped** + **60g** → Cook for 5 more minutes on a med/high heat stir occasionally remove from heat

Green Pepper   Tomatoes   Sultanas

Steam in a large casserole pot, layer half the rice, then the curry. Finish with the rest of the rice. Cover, steam on the lowest heat for 20 minutes, allow to rest for 5-10 minutes. SERVE with fresh coriander and plain yogurt

50g per Serving   **5g per Serving**
Plain Yogurt   +   Fresh Coriander

Large Casserole Pot

SERVE →

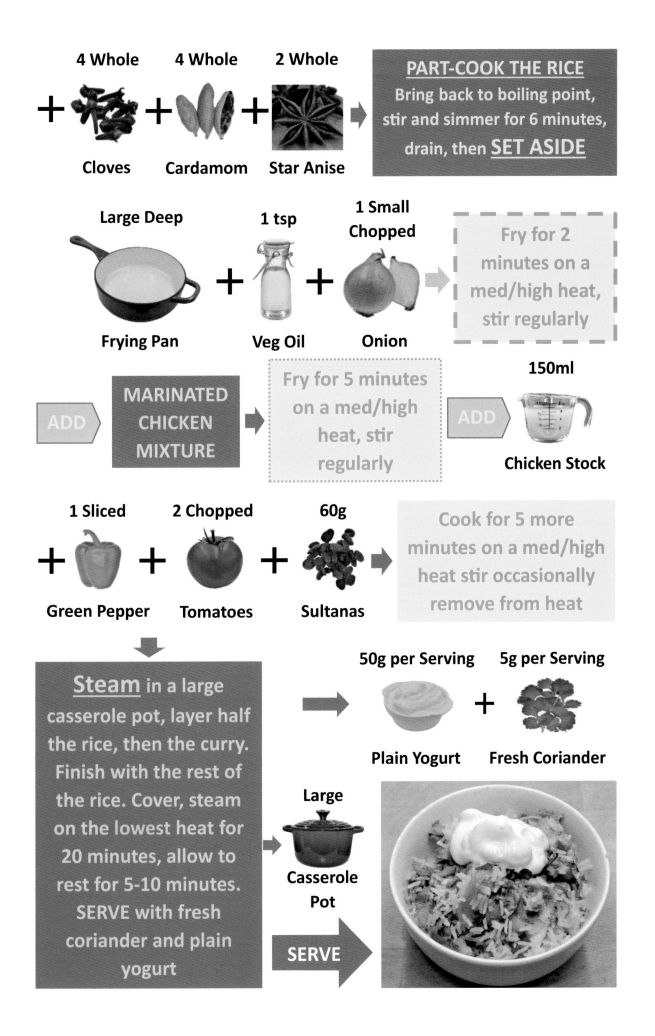

Mushroom Chow Mein
Ingredients

1.5 litres Boiling Water

300 grams Medium Egg Noodles

4 Tablespoons Vegetable Oil

1 Large Onion

8 Cloves Garlic

400g Chestnut Mushrooms

½ Teaspoon Black Pepper

100ml Vegetable Stock

4 Tablespoons Light Soy Sauce

4 Tablespoons Oyster Sauce

120 grams Spring Onions

140 grams Mangetout

200 grams Bean Sprouts

½ Teaspoon Five Spice

1 Tablespoon Toasted Sesame Oil

NOTES;

For vegan option omit the oyster sauce and replace the egg noodles for rice noodles.

When soaking the noodles and before setting aside in cold water, test them; they should have a slightly firm bite.

Chicken stock can be used.

Cooking individual portions is best as it keeps the wok hot avoiding soggy food.

Mushroom Chow Mein

Best stir-fried in individual portions to retain the heat in the wok. Divide the ingredients by four and cook individually . **Delicious dish. Serves 4**

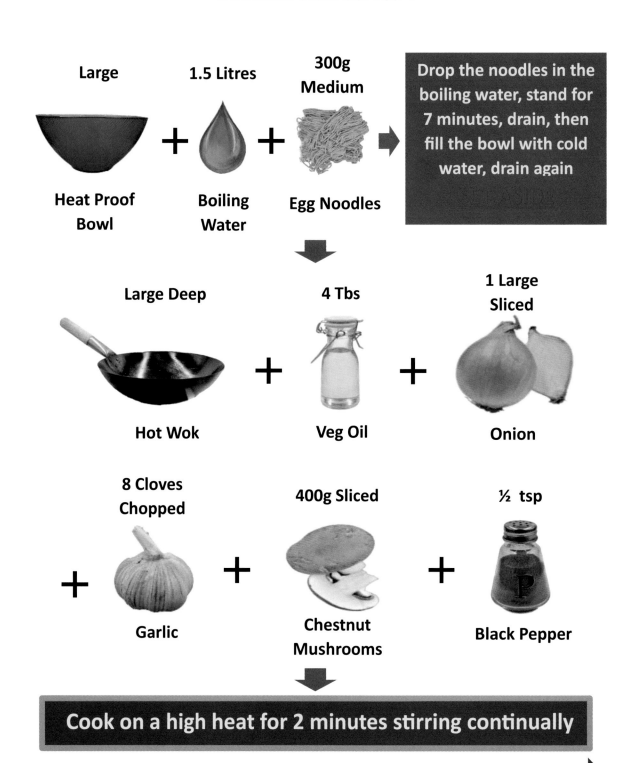

Large

1.5 Litres

300g Medium

Drop the noodles in the boiling water, stand for 7 minutes, drain, then fill the bowl with cold water, drain again

Heat Proof Bowl

Boiling Water

Egg Noodles

Large Deep

4 Tbs

1 Large Sliced

Hot Wok

Veg Oil

Onion

8 Cloves Chopped

400g Sliced

½ tsp

Garlic

Chestnut Mushrooms

Black Pepper

Cook on a high heat for 2 minutes stirring continually

ADD SET-ASIDE Cooked

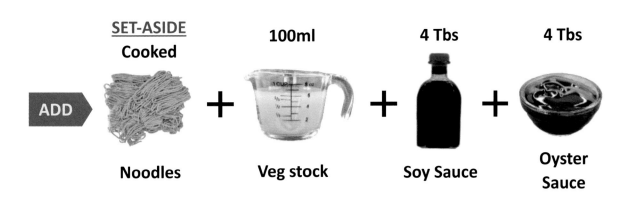

Noodles + 100ml Veg stock + 4 Tbs Soy Sauce + 4 Tbs Oyster Sauce

Heat through for 2 minutes stirring regularly

THEN ADD 120g Sliced Spring Onions + 140g Whole Mangetout + 200g Bean Sprouts + ½ tsp Five Spice

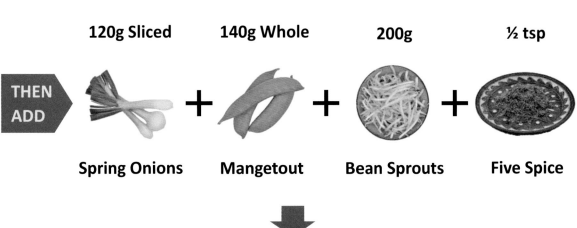

STIR IN SPRING ONIONS, MANGETOUT BEAN, FIVE SPICE AND BEAN SPROUTS. COOK FOR A FURTHER 2 MINUTES

Drizzle over

1 Tbs

Toasted sesame Oil

SERVE

39

Beef Stew and Dumplings

Ingredients

2 Tablespoons Olive Oil

2 Medium Onions

600 grams Beef (Chuck or Sirloin)

2 Thick Rashers of Back Bacon

2 Tablespoons Plain Flour

1 Teaspoon Salt

½ Teaspoon Ground Black Pepper

3 Large Carrots

1 Half (450g) Savoy Cabbage

400ml Beef Stock

600ml Water

180 grams Self Raising Flour

90 grams Shredded Vegetable Suet

1 Teaspoon Mixed Herbs

½ Teaspoon Salt

¼ Teaspoon Black Pepper

120 to 140ml Cold Water

NOTES;

For a vegan alternative, replace the meat with potatoes and swede, cut in large chunks and use a vegetable stock.

Depending on your preference add more water for more of a sauce.

When making dumplings slowly add the water to achieve the correct consistency, if you add too much water add a little flour, the dumplings should be slightly sticky.

Use vegetable suet.

Beef Stew and Dumplings

A truly tasty meal, not just a winters day dish.
Set oven to 180°c   Serves 5

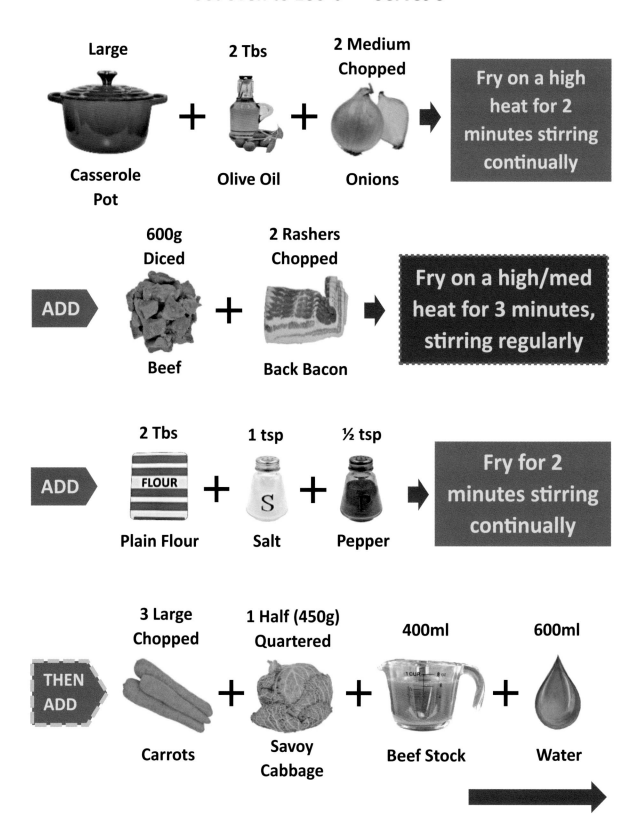

Large — Casserole Pot

2 Tbs — Olive Oil

2 Medium Chopped — Onions

Fry on a high heat for 2 minutes stirring continually

ADD — 600g Diced — Beef

2 Rashers Chopped — Back Bacon

Fry on a high/med heat for 3 minutes, stirring regularly

ADD — 2 Tbs — Plain Flour

1 tsp — Salt

½ tsp — Pepper

Fry for 2 minutes stirring continually

THEN ADD — 3 Large Chopped — Carrots

1 Half (450g) Quartered — Savoy Cabbage

400ml — Beef Stock

600ml — Water

Cover and cook in the oven for 1 ½ hours at 180°c

Prepare your dumplings → **Large** Mixing Bowl + **180g Sieved** Self-Raising Flour + **90g** Shredded Suet + **1 tsp** Mixed Herbs

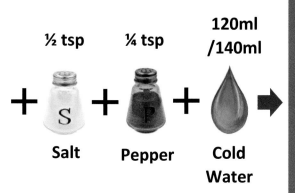

+ **½ tsp** Salt + **¼ tsp** Pepper + **120ml /140ml** Cold Water → Mix together, lightly knead on a floured surface by stretching firmly with the heal of your hand and folding in the edges, then bringing the mixture back together, repeat for 1 minute; your dough should be firm and slightly sticky. Makes 10 squash ball sized dumplings

Remove the stew from oven after 1½ hours, stir carefully, then place dumplings on top and continue to cook <u>uncovered</u> in the oven for 30 minutes, baste the dumplings with the juices halfway through cooking

Remove the stew from the oven and allow to stand for 10 minutes **SERVE** →

Spanish Omelette
Ingredients

Water for Potatoes

600 grams Potatoes

2 Tablespoons Olive Oil

1 Small Onion

3 Cloves Garlic

50 grams Chorizo

1 Red Pepper

Pinch of Salt

¼ Teaspoon Black Pepper

1 Teaspoon Oregano

Water for Peas

180 grams Peas

8 Large Eggs

150 grams Medium Cheddar Cheese

15 Cherry Tomatoes

1 Small Cucumber

1 Tablespoon Olive Oil

¼ Teaspoon Salt

¼ Teaspoon Black Pepper

NOTES;

For a vegetarian option replace the chorizo sausage with ¼ teaspoon sweet paprika.

Fresh peas need no boiling.

If you are not using an ovenproof frying pan, make sure the handle does not go under the grill.

Spanish Omelette

Easy omelette to make, you can make many variations.

Set grill to 220°c   Serves 4

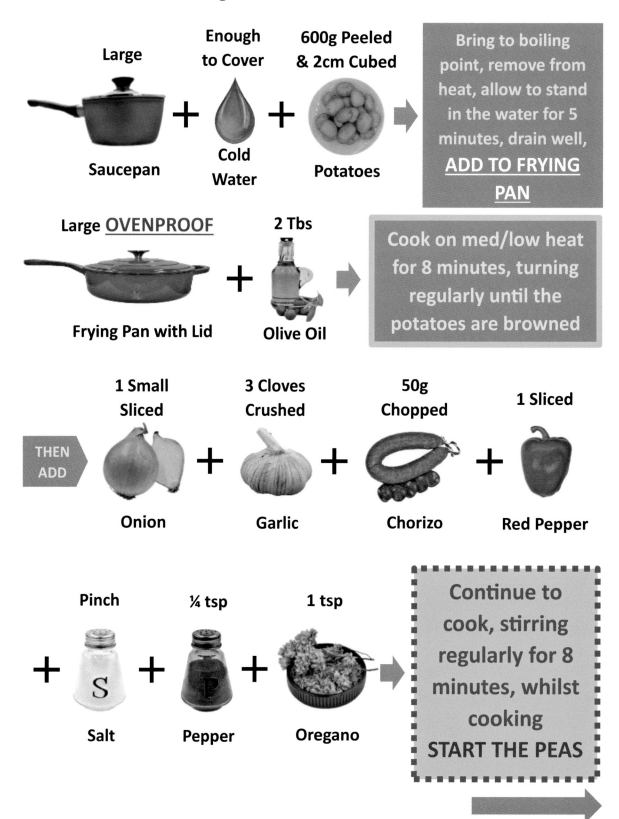

Large
Saucepan

+

Enough to Cover
Cold Water

+

600g Peeled & 2cm Cubed
Potatoes

→

Bring to boiling point, remove from heat, allow to stand in the water for 5 minutes, drain well, **ADD TO FRYING PAN**

Large OVENPROOF
Frying Pan with Lid

+

2 Tbs
Olive Oil

→

Cook on med/low heat for 8 minutes, turning regularly until the potatoes are browned

THEN ADD

1 Small Sliced
Onion

+

3 Cloves Crushed
Garlic

+

50g Chopped
Chorizo

+

1 Sliced
Red Pepper

+

Pinch
Salt

+

¼ tsp
Pepper

+

1 tsp
Oregano

→

Continue to cook, stirring regularly for 8 minutes, whilst cooking **START THE PEAS**

Small + **¾ Full** + **180g**

Saucepan   Boiling Water   Peas

Bring back to the boil, reduce heat to low, simmer for 2 minutes, drain, then add to the <u>frying pan</u>

Medium + **8 Large**

Mixing Bowl   Eggs

Beat the eggs for 10 seconds then ADD ➡

150g Grated

Cheddar Cheese

Add the beaten egg mixture to the frying pan and mix together

Cover and cook for 5 minutes on a low heat. Then uncover and place under a hot grill until lightly browned

MAKE SALAD ➡

Medium + **15 Halved** + **1 Small Chopped** + **1 tsp**

Bowl   Cherry Tomatoes   Cucumber   Olive Oil

+ **¼ tsp** + **¼ tsp**

Salt   Pepper

CUT OMELETTE INTO WEDGES AND SERVE WITH SALAD ➡

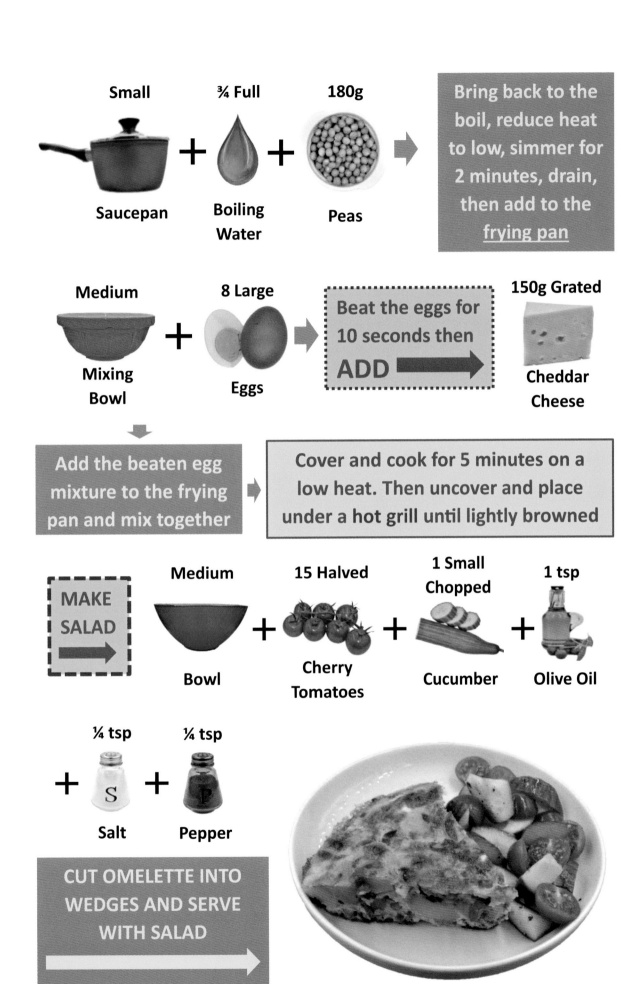

YOUR NOTES

Jacket Potatoes

Ingredients

4 Large Baking Potatoes
(300 grams Each)

1 Small Onion

2 Tins Haricot Beans (800 grams)

1 Carton Passata (500 grams)

1 Tablespoon Tomato Puree

300ml Vegetable Stock

2 Teaspoons Sugar

½ Teaspoon Salt

¼ Teaspoon Black Pepper

½ Teaspoon Dried Thyme

Pinch Ground Cinnamon

1 Teaspoon Malt Vinegar

1 Tablespoon Olive Oil

1 Small Onion

1 Tin Sweetcorn (140 grams)

1 Tin Tuna Drained (110 grams)

100 grams Mayonnaise

¼ Teaspoon Black Pepper

Water for Poaching Chicken

480 grams Chicken Breast

2 Teaspoons Mild Curry Powder

100 grams Mayonnaise

50 grams Mango Chutney

40 grams Sultanas

¼ Teaspoon Salt

¼ Teaspoon Black Pepper

NOTES;

An alternative to cooking potatoes in a casserole pot is to wrap the potatoes in foil, cook for 1 hour, then unwrap for the last ½ hour.

For a vegan alternative, use plant-based mayonnaise, replace the tuna with crushed chickpeas, and the chicken with soya chunks or similar.

Use tuna in spring water or in brine.

Jacket Potatoes

You can make limitless topping variations, here's three.

Set oven to 180°c   Serves 4

Large

Casserole Pot

+

4 Large (300g Each)

Baking Potatoes

Prick the potatoes all over with a fork. Cook in the oven, covered for 1 hour at 180°c, remove lid and cook for a further ½ an hour. The potatoes are <u>Ready to Serve</u>

Whilst the potatoes are cooking make your fillings

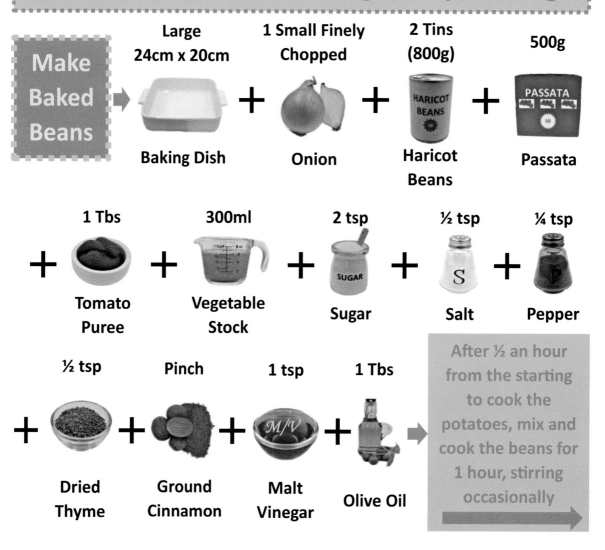

Make Baked Beans

Large 24cm x 20cm

Baking Dish

+

1 Small Finely Chopped

Onion

+

2 Tins (800g)

Haricot Beans

+

500g

Passata

+

1 Tbs

Tomato Puree

+

300ml

Vegetable Stock

+

2 tsp

Sugar

+

½ tsp

Salt

+

¼ tsp

Pepper

+

½ tsp

Dried Thyme

+

Pinch

Ground Cinnamon

+

1 tsp

Malt Vinegar

+

1 Tbs

Olive Oil

After ½ an hour from the starting to cook the potatoes, mix and cook the beans for 1 hour, stirring occasionally

Medium + **1 Small Finely Chopped** + **1 Tin (140g)**

Bowl + Onion + Sweetcorn

+ **1 Tin (110g)** + **100g** + **¼ tsp**

Tuna + Mayonnaise + Pepper

Mix together to make a Tuna, Sweetcorn and Onion topping

Medium + **½ Full** + **480g Diced (3cm)** → Bring to the boil, reduce heat to low and simmer for 6 minutes, then drain and place in mixing bowl → **Medium**

Saucepan + Water + Chicken Breast → Mixing Bowl

+ **2 tsp** + **100g** + **50g** + **40g** + **¼ tsp** + **¼ tsp**

Mild Curry Powder + Mayonnaise + Mango Chutney + Sultanas + Salt + Pepper

Mix together to make Coronation Chicken → Cheese can be added to any of these toppings →

Baked Beans   Tuna   Chicken

42

Tuna Niçoise salad
Ingredients

Water for Potatoes

600 grams New Potatoes

Boiling Water for French Beans

350 grams French Beans

Water for Eggs

4 Large Eggs

8 Tablespoons Olive Oil

1 Teaspoon Wholegrain Mustard

1 Teaspoon Lemon Juice

4 Teaspoons White Wine Vinegar

1 Tablespoon Honey

¼ Teaspoon Salt

2 Whole Little Gem Lettuces

4 Large Tomatoes

80 grams Kalamata Olives

2 Tablespoons Olive Oil

400 grams Fresh Tuna Steaks

NOTES;

Tinned tuna (in olive oil) can be used.

For vegan option leave out the tuna and replace with red kidney beans.

43

Tuna Niçoise salad

Light and delicious!   **Serves 4**

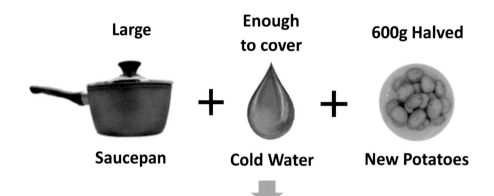

Large | Enough to cover | 600g Halved
Saucepan | Cold Water | New Potatoes

Bring the potatoes to boiling point, reduce heat to low and simmer for 10 minutes, drain and SET ASIDE

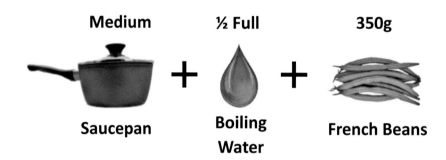

Medium | ½ Full | 350g
Saucepan | Boiling Water | French Beans

Bring back to the boil, reduce heat to low and simmer for 3 minutes, drain and SET ASIDE

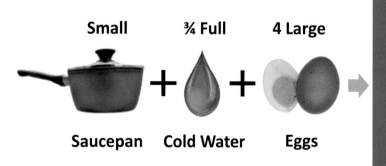

Small | ¾ Full | 4 Large
Saucepan | Cold Water | Eggs

Bring the eggs to boiling point, reduce heat to low, simmer for 8 minutes, drain and fill saucepan with cold water. Once eggs have cooled, peel and SET ASIDE

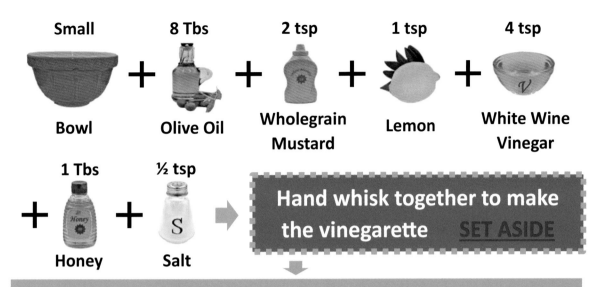

Small **Bowl** + 8 Tbs **Olive Oil** + 2 tsp **Wholegrain Mustard** + 1 tsp **Lemon** + 4 tsp **White Wine Vinegar**

+ 1 Tbs **Honey** + ½ tsp **Salt** →

Hand whisk together to make the vinegarette SET ASIDE

DIVIDE SALAD INGREDIENTS BY 4, BUILD THE SALAD

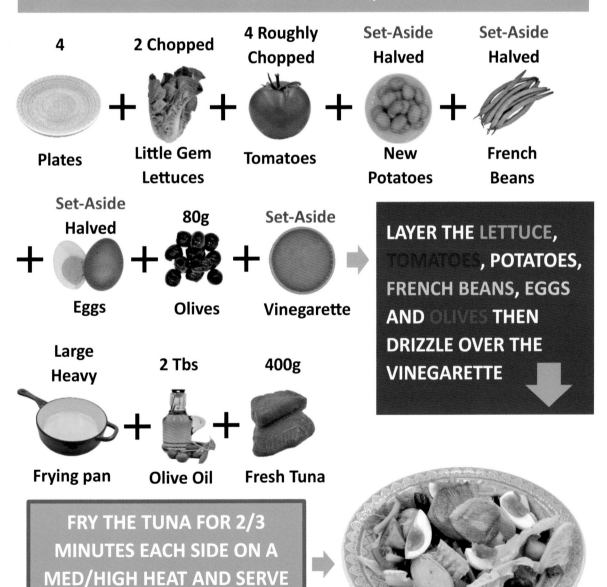

4 **Plates** + 2 Chopped **Little Gem Lettuces** + 4 Roughly Chopped **Tomatoes** + Set-Aside Halved **New Potatoes** + Set-Aside Halved **French Beans**

+ Set-Aside Halved **Eggs** + 80g **Olives** + Set-Aside **Vinegarette** →

LAYER THE LETTUCE, TOMATOES, POTATOES, FRENCH BEANS, EGGS AND OLIVES THEN DRIZZLE OVER THE VINEGARETTE

Large Heavy **Frying pan** + 2 Tbs **Olive Oil** + 400g **Fresh Tuna**

FRY THE TUNA FOR 2/3 MINUTES EACH SIDE ON A MED/HIGH HEAT AND SERVE ON TOP OF THE SALAD →

43

White Chicken Lasagne

Ingredients

2 Tablespoon Olive Oil

480 grams Chicken Breast

½ Teaspoon Salt

½ Teaspoon Black Pepper

2 Tablespoon Olive Oil

1 Small Onion

3 Cloves Garlic

150 grams Button Mushrooms

250 grams Spinach

4 Tablespoons Vegetable Oil

80 grams Plain Flour

800ml Whole Milk

100 grams Medium Cheddar

100 grams Mature Cheddar

¼ Teaspoon Ground Nutmeg

½ Teaspoon Black Pepper

180 grams Pasta Sheets

100 grams Medium Cheddar

100 grams Mozzarella

NOTES;

For a dairy free option use soya or oat milk; a 50-50 combination works well.

For vegan option replace the chicken with soya chunks.

Add a little more water to the chicken mixture if needed.

You can use individual pie dishes if you like and freeze some for another day.

White Chicken Lasagne

Great alternative to beef lasagne. Set oven to 220°c
Serves 5-6

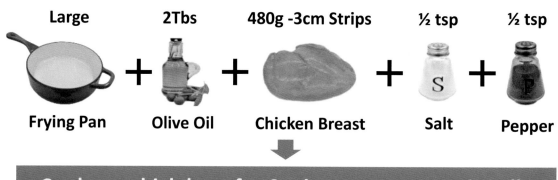

Large	2Tbs	480g -3cm Strips	½ tsp	½ tsp
Frying Pan	Olive Oil	Chicken Breast	Salt	Pepper

Cook on a high heat for 6 minutes turn occasionally until browned. SET ASIDE and, using the same pan

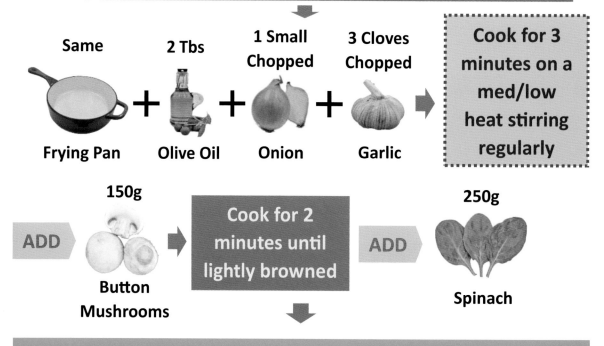

Same	2 Tbs	1 Small Chopped	3 Cloves Chopped	Cook for 3 minutes on a med/low heat stirring regularly
Frying Pan	Olive Oil	Onion	Garlic	

ADD — 150g **Button Mushrooms** → **Cook for 2 minutes until lightly browned** → **ADD** — 250g **Spinach**

Mix together with the chicken mixture and ➡ SET ASIDE

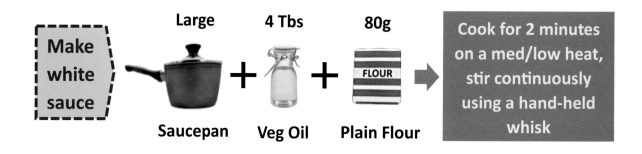

Make white sauce

Large	4 Tbs	80g	Cook for 2 minutes on a med/low heat, stir continuously using a hand-held whisk
Saucepan	Veg Oil	Plain Flour	

FLOUR

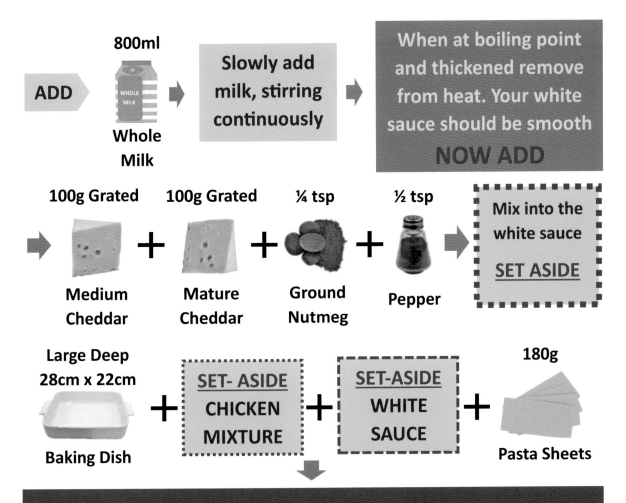

ADD → **800ml** Whole Milk → **Slowly add milk, stirring continuously** → **When at boiling point and thickened remove from heat. Your white sauce should be smooth NOW ADD**

→ **100g Grated** Medium Cheddar **+** **100g Grated** Mature Cheddar **+** **¼ tsp** Ground Nutmeg **+** **½ tsp** Pepper → **Mix into the white sauce SET ASIDE**

Large Deep 28cm x 22cm Baking Dish **+** **SET- ASIDE CHICKEN MIXTURE** **+** **SET-ASIDE WHITE SAUCE** **+** **180g** Pasta Sheets

Mix roughly two thirds of the white sauce with the chicken mixture. **BUILD THE LASAGNE:** first add to the dish a couple of spoons of the white sauce, then a layer of pasta sheets, next half of the chicken mixture, then pasta sheets, then the rest of the chicken mixture, then a layer of pasta sheets finishing with the remaining third of white sauce.

PLACE ON TOP 100g GRATED CHEDDAR CHEESE **+** 100G TORN MOZZARELLA

BAKE FOR 20 MINUTES AT 220°C

SERVE WITH BROCCOLI

Katsu curry

Ingredients

2 Tablespoons Vegetable Oil

1 Small Onion

4 Cloves Garlic

1 Medium Carrot

100 grams Butternut Squash

1 Tablespoon Medium Curry Powder

1 ½ Tablespoon Plain Flour

350ml Chicken Stock

250ml Coconut Milk

1 Tablespoon Sugar

1 Tablespoon Light Soy Sauce

750 grams Whole Chicken Breast

½ Teaspoon Salt

½ Teaspoon Black Pepper

Water for Rice (600ml)

300 grams Basmati Rice

1 Tin (340 grams) Sweetcorn

1 Whole Cucumber

1 Little Gem Lettuce

1 Large Carrot

NOTES;

For a vegan option replace chicken stock with vegetable stock and replace the chicken with a plant-based steak.

If not using coconut milk, increase carrots to 3 and use 300g butternut squash.

Blend or sieve the sauce.

Chicken can be coated in breadcrumbs by simply dusting in flour then dipping in beaten egg, finally coating in breadcrumbs.

Any salad stuff can be used.

Katsu curry

There are many variations of katsu; this one is delicious.

Set oven to 220°c   Serves 5

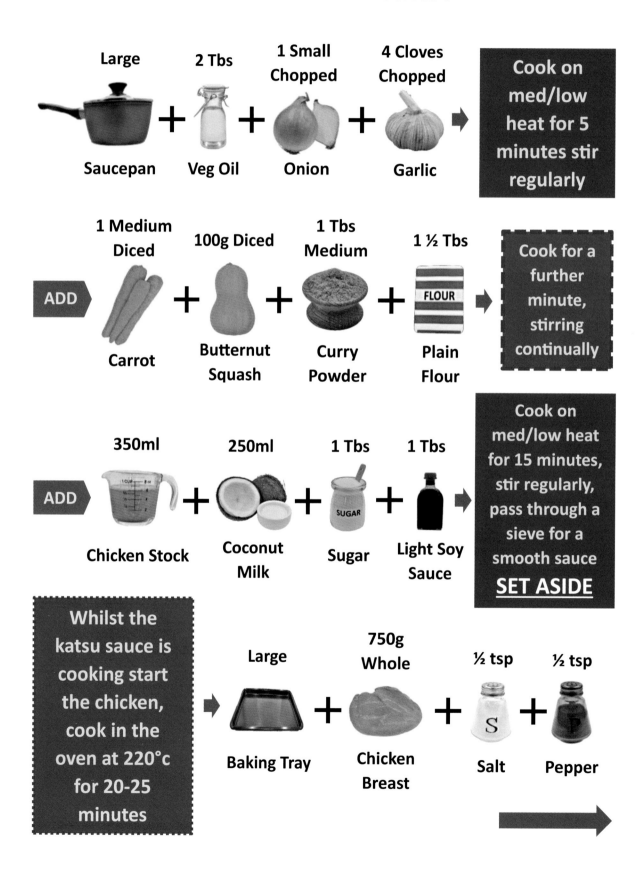

Large + 2 Tbs + 1 Small Chopped + 4 Cloves Chopped → Cook on med/low heat for 5 minutes stir regularly

Saucepan   Veg Oil   Onion   Garlic

ADD 1 Medium Diced + 100g Diced + 1 Tbs Medium + 1 ½ Tbs → Cook for a further minute, stirring continually

Carrot   Butternut Squash   Curry Powder   Plain Flour

ADD 350ml + 250ml + 1 Tbs + 1 Tbs → Cook on med/low heat for 15 minutes, stir regularly, pass through a sieve for a smooth sauce **SET ASIDE**

Chicken Stock   Coconut Milk   Sugar   Light Soy Sauce

Whilst the katsu sauce is cooking start the chicken, cook in the oven at 220°c for 20-25 minutes → Large + 750g Whole + ½ tsp + ½ tsp

Baking Tray   Chicken Breast   Salt   Pepper

Small   600ml   300g

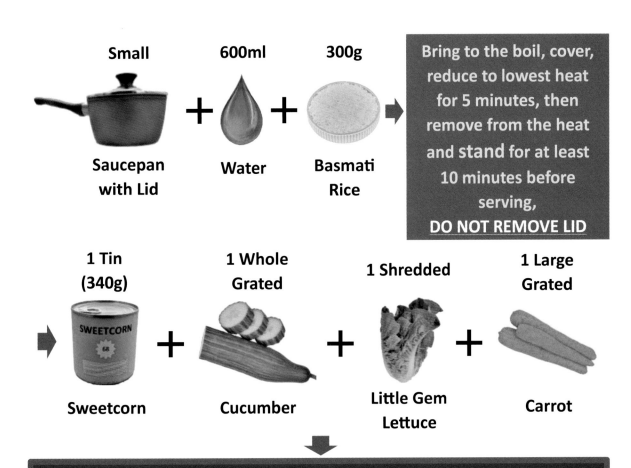

+   **+**

Saucepan with Lid   Water   Basmati Rice

Bring to the boil, cover, reduce to lowest heat for 5 minutes, then remove from the heat and **stand** for at least 10 minutes before serving,
DO NOT REMOVE LID

1 Tin (340g)   1 Whole Grated   1 Shredded   1 Large Grated

SWEETCORN

+   **+**   **+**

Sweetcorn   Cucumber   Little Gem Lettuce   Carrot

Arrange the salad in small piles on the plate, slice the chicken diagonally. Using a small, oiled ramakin or cup, fill with rice, compress the rice, turn out onto the plate and pour over some katsu sauce.

YOUR NOTES

Steak and Chips

Ingredients

Water for Potatoes

800 grams Potatoes

6 Tablespoons Plain Flour

3 Tablespoons Corn Flour

2 Teaspoons Bicarbonate of Soda

½ Teaspoon Salt

½ Teaspoon Black Pepper

130ml Cold Water

1 litre Vegetable Oil

1 Large Onion

2 Tablespoons Olive Oil

700 grams Fillet Steak

½ Teaspoon Salt

½ Teaspoon Black Pepper

4 Tomatoes

Water for Peas

300 grams Peas

NOTES;

The thickness of the steak can affect the cooking time; in this recipe I used 4cm thick steaks.

Fries should be about 1cm thick.

Use soda water or beer to replace bi-carb and water for the batter.

When placing the fries and the onion rings in the hot oil, turn off the heat, gently lower the fries and onion rings in the oil with a wide gauge sieve or slotted spoon, turn back on the heat once the fries and onion rings are in the oil.

For safety, keep the handle to the back of the stove.

For vegan option replace steak with a plant-based alternative.

Steak and Chips

Classic dish, delicious.

Set oven to 100°c   **Serves 4**

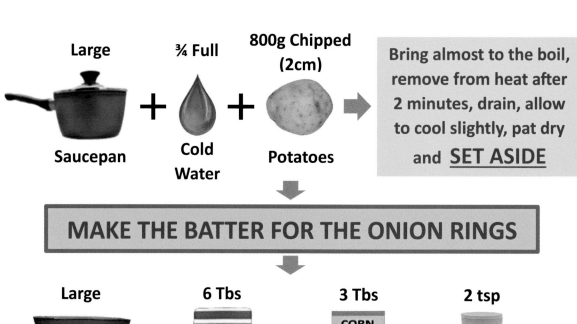

Large — Saucepan + ¾ Full — Cold Water + 800g Chipped (2cm) — Potatoes → Bring almost to the boil, remove from heat after 2 minutes, drain, allow to cool slightly, pat dry and **SET ASIDE**

MAKE THE BATTER FOR THE ONION RINGS

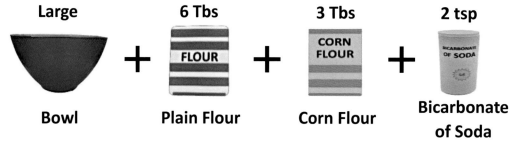

Large — Bowl + 6 Tbs — Plain Flour + 3 Tbs — Corn Flour + 2 tsp — Bicarbonate of Soda

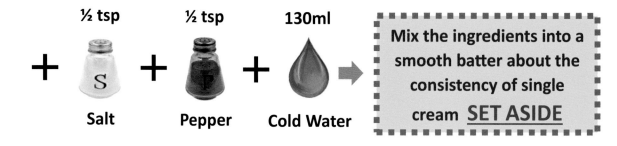

+ ½ tsp — Salt + ½ tsp — Pepper + 130ml — Cold Water → Mix the ingredients into a smooth batter about the consistency of single cream **SET ASIDE**

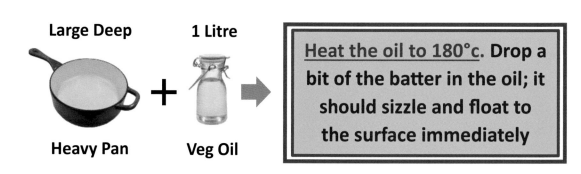

Large Deep — Heavy Pan + 1 Litre — Veg Oil → Heat the oil to 180°c. Drop a bit of the batter in the oil; it should sizzle and float to the surface immediately

1 Large Sliced 1cm Rings

SET-ASIDE

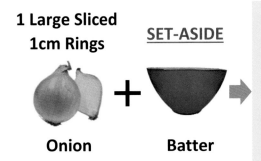

Onion + **Batter** →

Dip onion rings into the batter using tongs and gently place in the hot oil. Don't overcrowd the pan. Cook for 2 minutes each side or when golden in colour. Remove from the oil and place on kitchen paper to soak up excess oil then put them in the oven to keep warm.

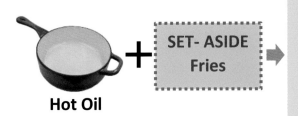

Hot Oil + **SET-ASIDE Fries** →

In batches, using a slotted spoon or wide gauge sieve, lower the fries in the oil and fry for 5-6 minutes. Remove, drain on kitchen paper, then put them in the oven to keep warm.

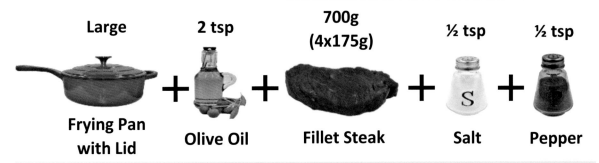

Large + **2 tsp** + **700g (4x175g)** + **½ tsp** + **½ tsp**

Frying Pan with Lid   **Olive Oil**   **Fillet Steak**   **Salt**   **Pepper**

Fry for 4 minutes each side (covered) for medium rare, 6 minutes per side for well-done   **ADD TO THE SAME PAN (FOR 4 MINUTES)**

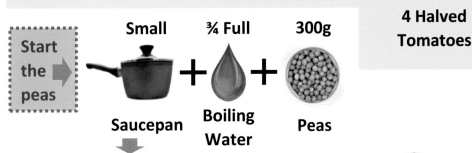

Start the peas → **Small** + **¾ Full** + **300g**

4 Halved Tomatoes →

Saucepan   **Boiling Water**   **Peas**

Bring back to the boil, cook for 2 minutes, drain the peas and serve with the steak, fries, onion rings and tomatoes →

YOUR NOTES

BBQ Chicken and Potato Salad

Ingredients

Water for Potatoes

650 grams New Potatoes

1 Tablespoon Salt

1 Tablespoon Olive Oil

1 Large Onion

3 Cloves Garlic

80 grams Light Muscovado Sugar

180ml Tomato Ketchup

3 Tablespoons Malt Vinegar

¼ Teaspoon Ground Nutmeg

½ Teaspoon Sweet Paprika

½ Teaspoon Salt

½ Teaspoon Black Pepper

1 Tablespoon Corn Flour

200ml Cold Water

1kg Chicken Thighs (skin on)

2 Teaspoons White Wine Vinegar

50 grams Spring Onions

100ml Mayonnaise

¼ Teaspoon Black Pepper

Water for Sweetcorn

4 Cobs of Sweetcorn

1 Teaspoon Salt

Knob of Butter

NOTES;

For a vegan alternative, use vegan mayonnaise and soya or mushroom protein fillets instead of the chicken.

If you have time marinate the chicken in the BBQ sauce for a couple of hours.

BBQ Chicken and Potato Salad

A dish popular in the USA.   Set oven to 200°c

Serves 5

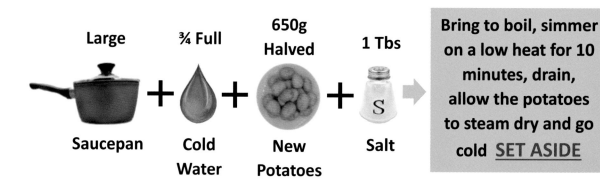

Large	¾ Full	650g Halved	1 Tbs	
Saucepan	+ Cold Water	+ New Potatoes	+ Salt	Bring to boil, simmer on a low heat for 10 minutes, drain, allow the potatoes to steam dry and go cold SET ASIDE

Whilst the potatoes are cooling start the BBQ sauce

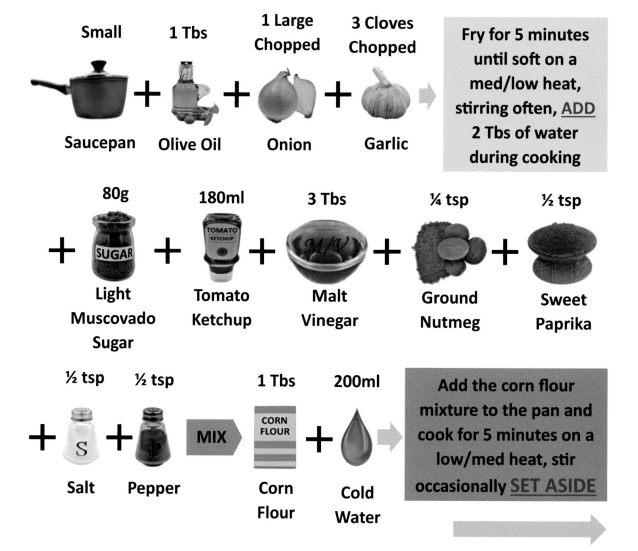

Small	1 Tbs	1 Large Chopped	3 Cloves Chopped	
Saucepan	+ Olive Oil	+ Onion	+ Garlic	Fry for 5 minutes until soft on a med/low heat, stirring often, ADD 2 Tbs of water during cooking

80g	180ml	3 Tbs	¼ tsp	½ tsp
+ Light Muscovado Sugar	+ Tomato Ketchup	+ Malt Vinegar	+ Ground Nutmeg	+ Sweet Paprika

½ tsp	½ tsp		1 Tbs	200ml	
+ Salt	+ Pepper	MIX	Corn Flour	+ Cold Water	Add the corn flour mixture to the pan and cook for 5 minutes on a low/med heat, stir occasionally SET ASIDE

Large   **SET-ASIDE**   **1kg**

Baking Tray   **+**   BBQ Sauce   **+**   Chicken Thighs

Coat the chicken in the BBQ Sauce, cover with foil, roast for 30 minutes at 200°c, remove foil and roast for a further 15 minutes

Medium   **Cooked**   **2 tsp**   **50g Chopped**   **100ml**   **¼ tsp**

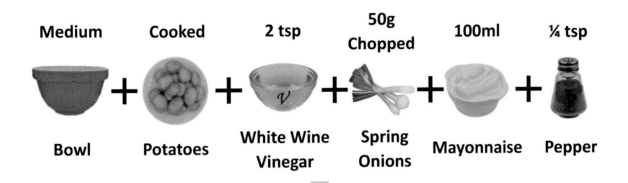

Bowl **+** Potatoes **+** White Wine Vinegar **+** Spring Onions **+** Mayonnaise **+** Pepper

MIX TOGETHER AND SET ASIDE, START THE SWEETCORN 5 MINUTES BEFORE THE CHICKEN IS READY

Large   **¾ Full**   **4 Cobs**   **1 tsp**

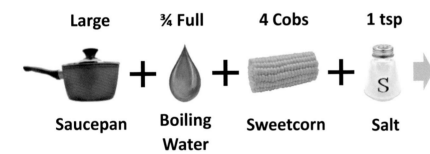

Saucepan **+** Boiling Water **+** Sweetcorn **+** Salt

Bring back to the boil, simmer for 4 minutes, drain. Add a knob of butter to the pan to coat the corn

BRING TOGETHER THE CHICKEN, POTATO SALAD AND SWEETCORN

SERVE

47

YOUR NOTES

Chicken Pasta

Ingredients

3 Tablespoons Olive Oil

1 Large Onion

4 Cloves Garlic

1 Large Carrot

100g Mushrooms

1 Stick Celery

2 Teaspoons Sugar

½ Teaspoon Black Pepper

1 Tablespoon Tomato Puree

600 grams Chicken Breast

6 Large Tomatoes

400ml Chicken stock

Juice of ½ a Lemon

½ Teaspoon Salt

Water for Pasta

450g Fusilli

NOTES;

Add more water for a wetter sauce.

For vegan option replace meat with soya chunks and stock with vegetable stock.

Chicken Pasta

Delicious, my kids love it.   Serves 5

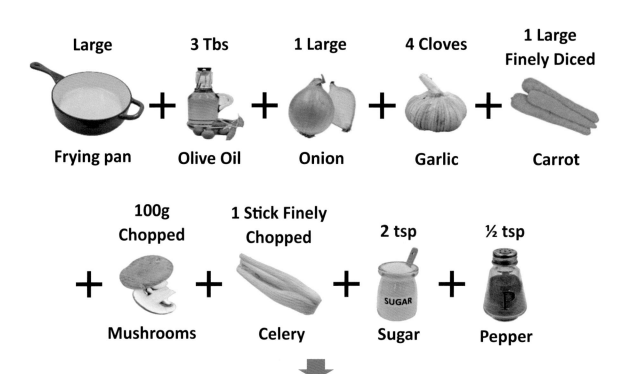

Large	3 Tbs	1 Large	4 Cloves	1 Large Finely Diced
Frying pan	Olive Oil	Onion	Garlic	Carrot

100g Chopped	1 Stick Finely Chopped	2 tsp	½ tsp
Mushrooms	Celery	Sugar	Pepper

Fry on med/low heat for 5 min stirring frequently

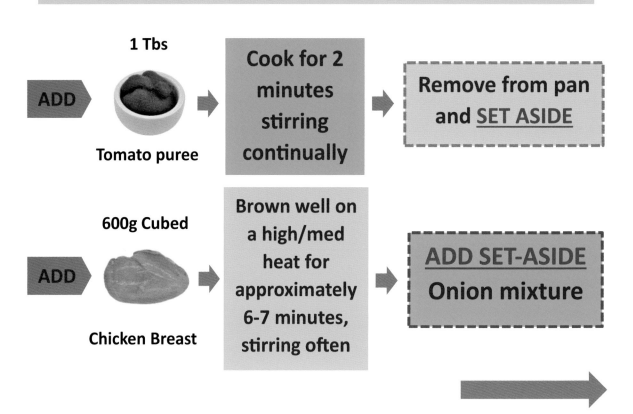

ADD — 1 Tbs — Tomato puree → **Cook for 2 minutes stirring continually** → **Remove from pan and SET ASIDE**

ADD — 600g Cubed — Chicken Breast → **Brown well on a high/med heat for approximately 6-7 minutes, stirring often** → **ADD SET-ASIDE Onion mixture**

48

ADD

6 Large Chopped	400ml	Juice of ½	½ tsp
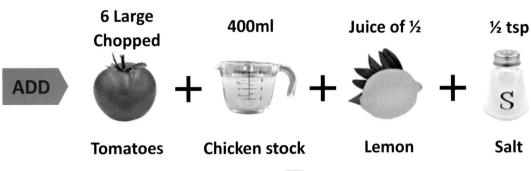
Tomatoes	+ Chicken stock	+ Lemon	+ Salt

Cook on med/low heat for 15 minutes, stir occasionally while the sauce is cooking, start the pasta

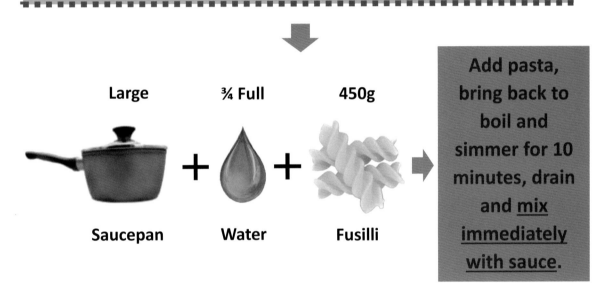

Large	¾ Full	450g	Add pasta, bring back to boil and simmer for 10 minutes, drain and **mix immediately with sauce**.
Saucepan	+ Water	+ Fusilli	

SERVE

Add a grated cheese of your choice

48

Sweet and Sour Prawn Noodles
Ingredients

3 Tablespoons Sake

180ml Tomato Ketchup

2 Teaspoons Light Soy Sauce

4 Tablespoons Light Brown Sugar

200ml Pineapple Juice

1 Tablespoon Corn Flour

Boiling Water for Noodles

300 grams Medium Egg Noodles

4 Tablespoons Vegetable Oil

1 Large Onion

2 Teaspoons Garlic Puree

2 Teaspoons Ginger Puree

1 Large Carrot

200 grams Button Mushrooms

260 grams Raw King Prawns

½ Teaspoon Salt

¼ Teaspoon Black Pepper

200 grams Bean Sprouts

1 Bunch Spring Onions

NOTES;

For a vegan option replace the egg noodles for rice noodles or even spaghetti. Replace prawns with tofu.

Cooking in individual portions is best when stir-frying.

Use any rice wine.

Sweet and Sour Prawn Noodles

Easy sweet and sour sauce, you can make many variations using the sauce.   Serves 4

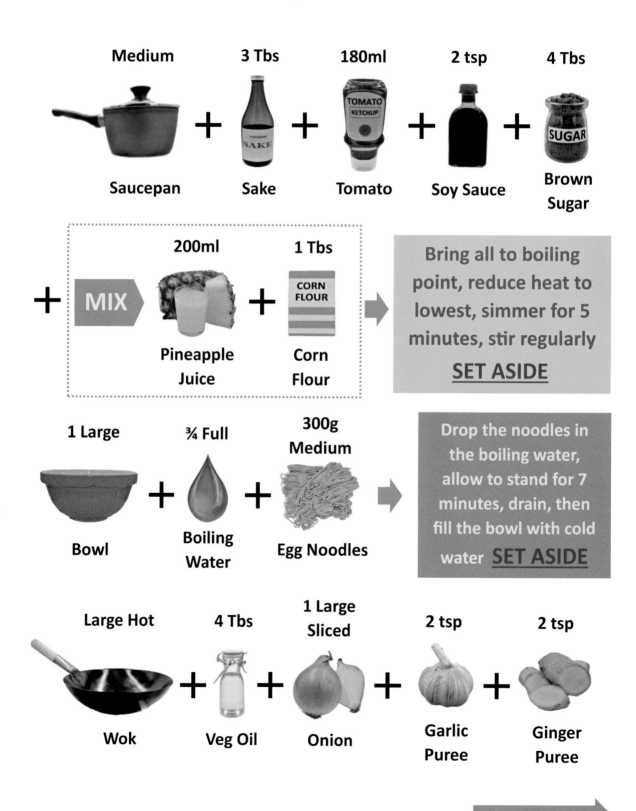

Medium + 3 Tbs + 180ml + 2 tsp + 4 Tbs

Saucepan   Sake   Tomato   Soy Sauce   Brown Sugar

+ MIX → 200ml + 1 Tbs

Pineapple Juice   Corn Flour

Bring all to boiling point, reduce heat to lowest, simmer for 5 minutes, stir regularly **SET ASIDE**

1 Large + ¾ Full + 300g Medium

Bowl   Boiling Water   Egg Noodles

Drop the noodles in the boiling water, allow to stand for 7 minutes, drain, then fill the bowl with cold water **SET ASIDE**

Large Hot + 4 Tbs + 1 Large Sliced + 2 tsp + 2 tsp

Wok   Veg Oil   Onion   Garlic Puree   Ginger Puree

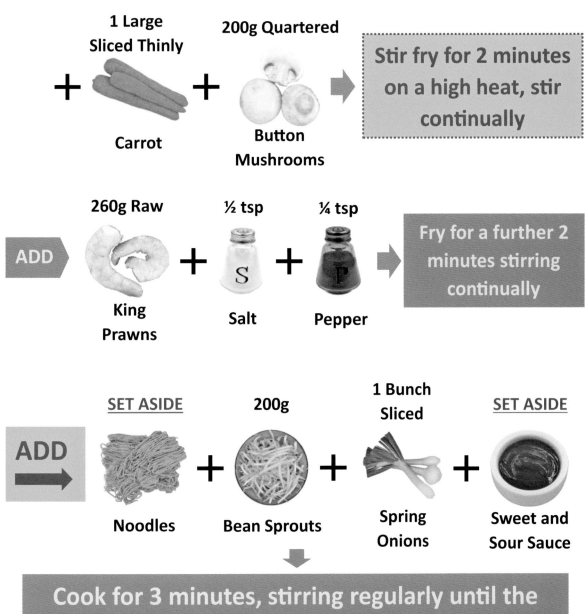

1 Large Sliced Thinly + Carrot + **200g Quartered** Button Mushrooms → Stir fry for 2 minutes on a high heat, stir continually

ADD **260g Raw** King Prawns + **½ tsp** Salt + **¼ tsp** Pepper → Fry for a further 2 minutes stirring continually

ADD SET ASIDE Noodles + **200g** Bean Sprouts + **1 Bunch Sliced** Spring Onions + SET ASIDE Sweet and Sour Sauce

Cook for 3 minutes, stirring regularly until the noodles are heated through

SERVE →

Fish Cakes and Apple Salad

Ingredients

Water for Potatoes

700 grams Potatoes

Water for Cod

250 grams Cod Fillet

1 Tablespoon Olive Oil

1 Small Onion

2 Cloves Garlic

1 Small Green Pepper

180 grams Raw king Prawns

1 Mild Green Chilli

20 grams Fresh Coriander

½ Teaspoon Salt

¼ Teaspoon White Pepper

Flour for Dusting

1 Tablespoon Olive Oil

3 Gala Apples

3 Tablespoons Honey

Juice of ½ a Lemon

1 Little Gem Lettuce (150 grams)

NOTES;

Tuna fish and white crab meat is a good combination instead of the cod and prawn.

For a vegan option use a dairy free butter and replace the fish with puy lentils or a small pulse, like black beans.

Be careful when turning the fish cakes.

50

Fish Cakes and Apple Salad

A light, delicious dinner.   Serves 4

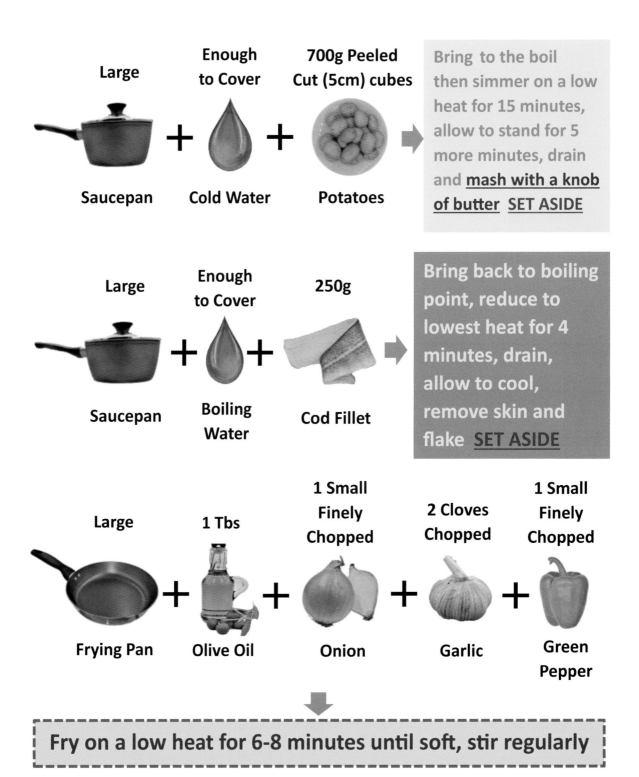

Large + **Enough to Cover** + **700g Peeled Cut (5cm) cubes**

Saucepan   Cold Water   Potatoes

Bring to the boil then simmer on a low heat for 15 minutes, allow to stand for 5 more minutes, drain and **mash with a knob of butter** SET ASIDE

Large + **Enough to Cover** + **250g**

Saucepan   Boiling Water   Cod Fillet

Bring back to boiling point, reduce to lowest heat for 4 minutes, drain, allow to cool, remove skin and flake **SET ASIDE**

Large + **1 Tbs** + **1 Small Finely Chopped** + **2 Cloves Chopped** + **1 Small Finely Chopped**

Frying Pan   Olive Oil   Onion   Garlic   Green Pepper

Fry on a low heat for 6-8 minutes until soft, stir regularly

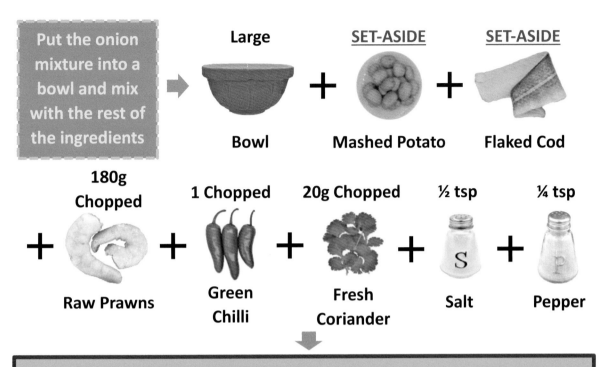

Put the onion mixture into a bowl and mix with the rest of the ingredients ➔

Large Bowl **+** **SET-ASIDE** Mashed Potato **+** **SET-ASIDE** Flaked Cod

+ **180g Chopped** Raw Prawns **+** **1 Chopped** Green Chilli **+** **20g Chopped** Fresh Coriander **+** **½ tsp** Salt **+** **¼ tsp** Pepper

⬇

Make into patties with your hands, each patty should be weighed at 160 grams. Dust each patty with flour before frying.

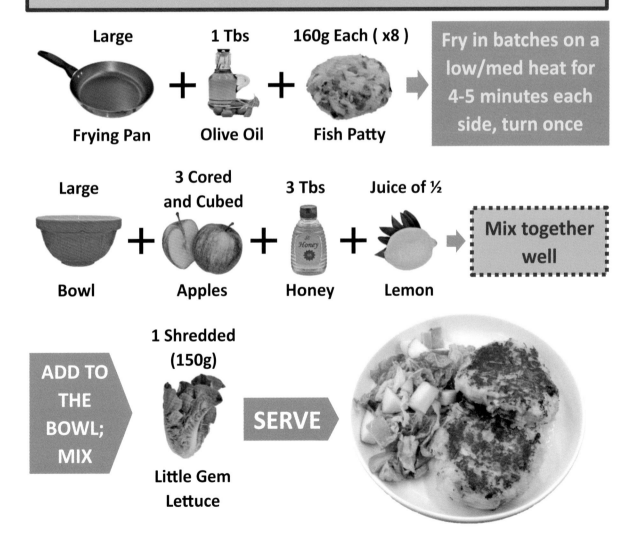

Large Frying Pan **+** **1 Tbs** Olive Oil **+** **160g Each (x8)** Fish Patty ➔ Fry in batches on a low/med heat for 4-5 minutes each side, turn once

Large Bowl **+** **3 Cored and Cubed** Apples **+** **3 Tbs** Honey **+** **Juice of ½** Lemon ➔ Mix together well

ADD TO THE BOWL; MIX ➔ **1 Shredded (150g)** Little Gem Lettuce SERVE ➔

Roti Chicken 'n' Potato
Ingredients

1 Tablespoon Vegetable Oil

650 grams Chicken Breast

1 Tablespoon Vegetable Oil

1 Large Onion

4 Cloves Garlic

3 Tablespoons Mild Curry Powder

600 grams Potatoes

½ Teaspoon Salt

½ Teaspoon Black Pepper

150ml Chicken Stock

1 Small Cucumber

240 grams Cherry Tomatoes

1 Medium Avocado

2 Small Shallots

Juice of half a Lemon

1 Tablespoon Honey

8 Teaspoons of Butter

8 Large Roti Skins (or Flour Wraps)

NOTES;

For a vegan option, replace the chicken with chickpeas and use a vegetable stock.

Use a vegan butter or vegetable oil.

Add chilli peppers for extra spice.

Serve with plain yogurt.

If you cannot find roti skins then any thin wrap can be used, even pita breads.

Roti Chicken 'n' Potato

A Caribbean inspired dish, enjoy!   **Serves 4**

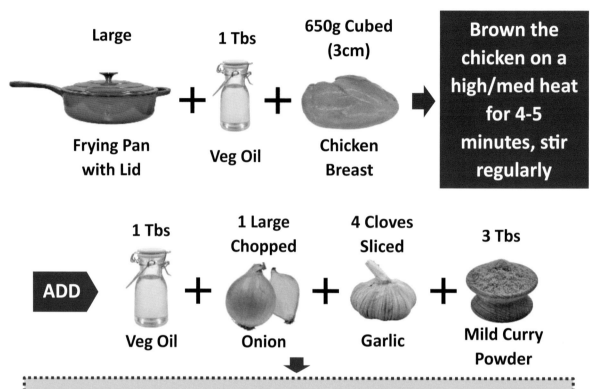

Large — **Frying Pan with Lid**

1 Tbs — **Veg Oil**

650g Cubed (3cm) — **Chicken Breast**

Brown the chicken on a high/med heat for 4-5 minutes, stir regularly

ADD 1 Tbs **Veg Oil** + 1 Large Chopped **Onion** + 4 Cloves Sliced **Garlic** + 3 Tbs **Mild Curry Powder**

Reduce heat to med/low and cook for 4 minutes stirring regularly

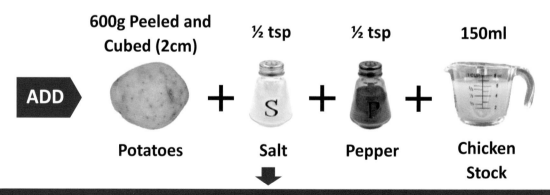

ADD 600g Peeled and Cubed (2cm) **Potatoes** + ½ tsp **Salt** + ½ tsp **Pepper** + 150ml **Chicken Stock**

Cover and cook on a med/low heat for 20 minutes until all of the water has been absorbed, stirring occasionally. SET ASIDE

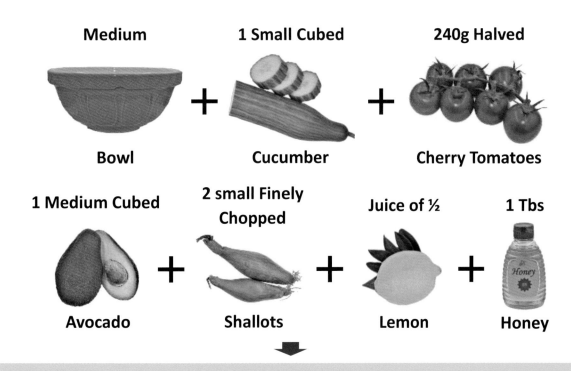

Medium

Bowl

1 Small Cubed

Cucumber

240g Halved

Cherry Tomatoes

1 Medium Cubed

Avocado

2 small Finely Chopped

Shallots

Juice of ½

Lemon

1 Tbs

Honey

Slice the cucumber, halve the tomatoes, cube the avocado, chop the shallots, pour over the lemon juice and drizzle the honey then mix well, your salad is ready to serve

Large

Frying Pan

1 tsp per Skin

Butter

8

Roti Skins

Fry each skin 20 seconds each side, on a high heat. Spoon the filling down the centre or the skin, roll or fold to create a parcel or tube SERVE

West Country Pasties
Ingredients

360 grams Strong White Bread Flour

100 grams Butter

80 grams Lard

¼ Teaspoon Salt

90ml Chilled Water

1 Tablespoon Olive Oil

375 grams Minced Beef

1 Medium Potato (250 grams)

1 Medium Carrot (120 grams)

1 Small Onion

1 Stick of Celery

1 Tablespoon Plain Flour

200ml Beef Stock

½ Teaspoon Salt

½ Teaspoon Black Pepper

1 Small Egg Yolk

NOTES;

Firm butter and lard, not too soft, not hard.

Use plenty of flour when rolling pastry.

Wet the closing edge of the pasty, when crimping together.

West Country Pasties

Making the pastry yourself is easy easy easy. I like serving the pasties with baked beans.   Set oven to 180°c

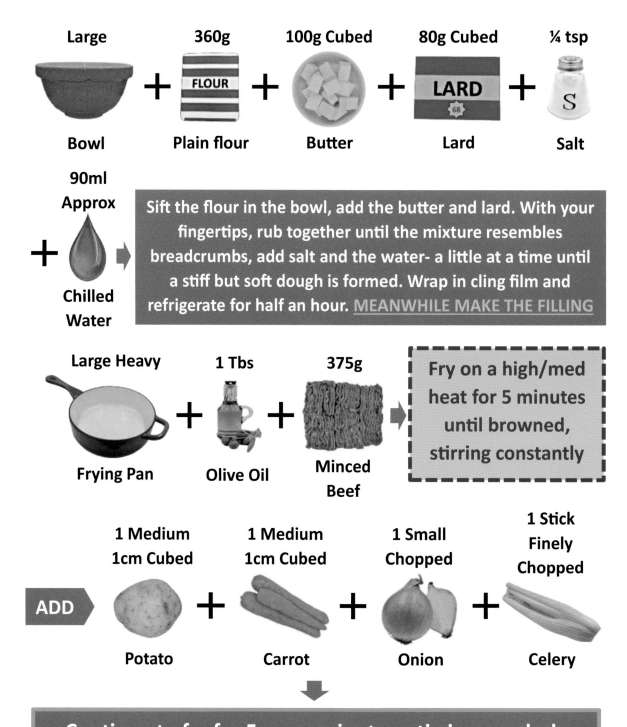

Large	360g	100g Cubed	80g Cubed	¼ tsp
Bowl	Plain flour	Butter	Lard	Salt

90ml Approx

Chilled Water

Sift the flour in the bowl, add the butter and lard. With your fingertips, rub together until the mixture resembles breadcrumbs, add salt and the water- a little at a time until a stiff but soft dough is formed. Wrap in cling film and refrigerate for half an hour. MEANWHILE MAKE THE FILLING

Large Heavy	1 Tbs	375g
Frying Pan	Olive Oil	Minced Beef

Fry on a high/med heat for 5 minutes until browned, stirring constantly

ADD

1 Medium 1cm Cubed	1 Medium 1cm Cubed	1 Small Chopped	1 Stick Finely Chopped
Potato	Carrot	Onion	Celery

Continue to fry for 5 more minutes, stirring regularly

ADD → **1 Tbs** Plain Flour → Cook on a medium heat for 1 minute, stirring constantly → **ADD** → **150ml** Beef Stock

½ tsp Salt **+** **½ tsp** Pepper → Cook for 15 minutes, on a low/med heat, stirring occasionally SET ASIDE allowing to cool

Weigh the dough, then divide into six parts, (approx. 100g each) form into balls. Flour the surface and rolling pin and roll out, turning and flouring regularly forming a rough circle about 20cm in diameter and about 2-3mm in thickness. Divide the meat mixture into sixths and pile onto the pastry circles. Bring up the edges to the top of the meat piles and crimp together with your fingers until completely sealed, then place a small slit either side of the pasty to allow the steam to escape during cooking

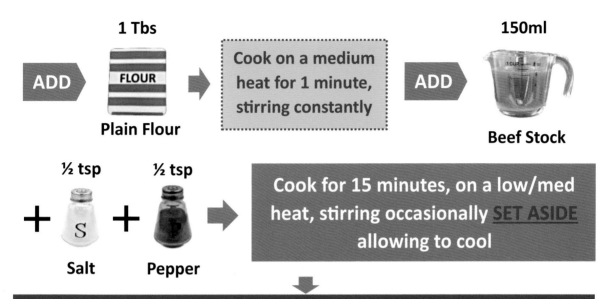

Large Baking Tray **+** **Enough to cover** Baking Paper → **Small** Bowl **+** **1 Small** Egg Yolk

Cover the tray with the paper and arrange the pasties on the tray, brush with beaten egg yolk Bake in the centre of the oven at 180°c for 25 minutes →

Toad in the Hole

Ingredients

115 grams Plain Flour

2 Medium Eggs

220ml Whole Milk

2 Tablespoons Melted Butter

¼ Teaspoon Salt

1 Tablespoon Vegetable Oil

8 Sausages (480 grams)

1kg Potatoes

Water for Potatoes

1 Teaspoon Salt

2 Tablespoons Vegetable Oil

1 Small Onion

2 Cloves Garlic

2 Tablespoons Plain Flour

450ml Beef Stock

Pinch Salt

Pinch Black Pepper

Water for Broccoli

1 Head of Broccoli (300 grams)

NOTES;

Buy a good quality sausage.

Be careful pouring the batter into the hot oil.

For a vegetarian option, use plant-based sausages and butter.

Use vegetable stock.

Toad in the Hole

Always a good choice. Set oven at 220°c.
Serves 4

Large — Bowl

115g Sieved — Plain Flour

2 Medium — Eggs

220ml — Whole Milk

2 Tbs Melted — Butter

¼ tsp — Salt

Whisk the ingredients together into a thin batter **SET ASIDE FOR AT LEAST 30 MINUTES**

Medium, Deep (26cm x 36cm) — Baking Tray

1 Tbs — Veg Oil

8 (480g) — Sausages

Coat the sausages with oil and roast in the oven for 5 minutes at 220°c

Remove the sausages from the oven and pour over the batter and bake for 25 minutes at 220°c, then reduce the heat to 180°c and continue to bake for a further 10 minutes. Remove from the oven. The toad in the hole is ready to serve.

Large | 1kg Peeled and Halved | Enough to Cover | 1 tsp

Saucepan + Potatoes + Water + Salt →

Bring to the boil, reduce heat to low and simmer for 15-20 until cooked through **SET ASIDE**

WHILST THE POTATOES ARE COOKING START THE GRAVY AND BROCCOLI

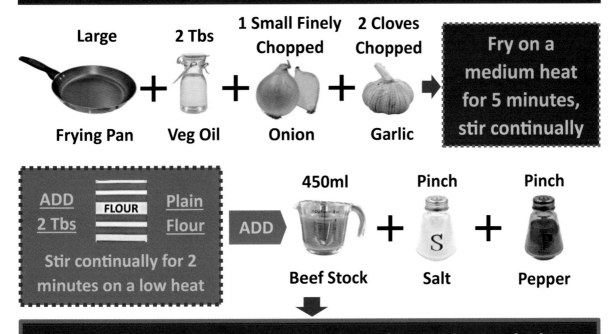

Large | 2 Tbs | 1 Small Finely Chopped | 2 Cloves Chopped

Frying Pan + Veg Oil + Onion + Garlic →

Fry on a medium heat for 5 minutes, stir continually

ADD 2 Tbs **FLOUR** Plain Flour

Stir continually for 2 minutes on a low heat

ADD →

450ml | Pinch | Pinch

Beef Stock + Salt + Pepper

Cook for 5 minutes on a medium heat stir regularly

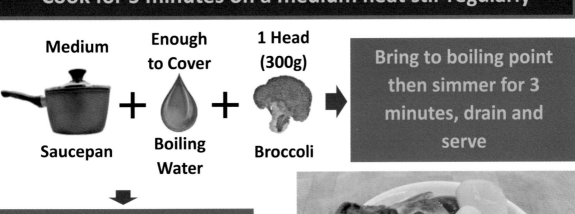

Medium | Enough to Cover | 1 Head (300g)

Saucepan + Boiling Water + Broccoli →

Bring to boiling point then simmer for 3 minutes, drain and serve

Bring the toad in the hole, potatoes and broccoli together and serve with the gravy →

Chicken Kebabs
Ingredients

3 Tablespoon Olive Oil

500g Chicken Breast

4 Cloves Garlic

Juice of 1 Lemon

2 Teaspoons Fresh Thyme

½ Teaspoon Salt

½ Teaspoon Black Pepper

1 Red Pepper

1 Large Onion

1 Green Pepper

250g Greek Yogurt

½ a Cucumber

½ Teaspoon Garlic Puree

2 Teaspoons Lemon Juice

Pinch of Salt

Pinch of Black Pepper

8 Large Pita Bread

1 Little Gem Lettuce

4 Tomatoes

1 Cucumber

160g Gherkins

NOTES;

Soak the skewers in water for 1 hour. Alternatively, use metal skewers.

Any vegetable can be used; if using root vegetables, use thinly sliced or part-boiled.

For a vegan option replace the meat with chestnut mushrooms or soya chunks, and use a vegan yogurt instead of Greek yogurt.

The kebabs can be oven-baked: wrap in foil and bake for 20 minutes at 220°c, unwrap and continue to bake for a further 5 minutes.

Chicken Kebabs

Really easy and really tasty, serve with tzatziki.
Serves 4

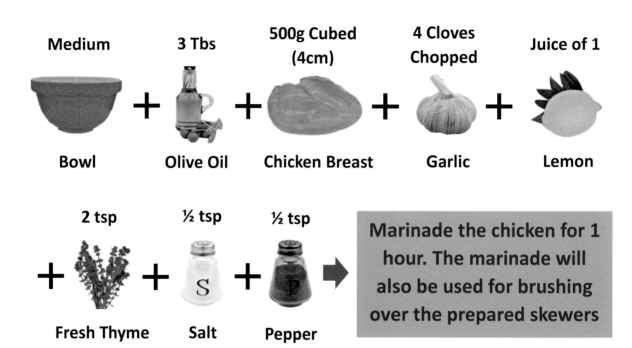

Medium + 3 Tbs + 500g Cubed (4cm) + 4 Cloves Chopped + Juice of 1

Bowl + Olive Oil + Chicken Breast + Garlic + Lemon

2 tsp + ½ tsp + ½ tsp → Marinade the chicken for 1 hour. The marinade will also be used for brushing over the prepared skewers

Fresh Thyme + Salt + Pepper

PREPARE THE SKEWERS FOR GRILLING

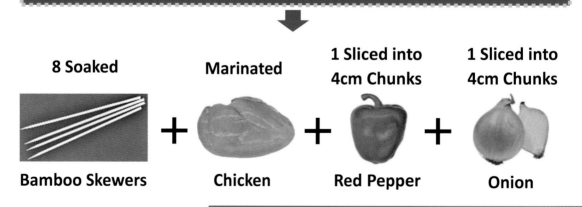

8 Soaked + Marinated + 1 Sliced into 4cm Chunks + 1 Sliced into 4cm Chunks

Bamboo Skewers + Chicken + Red Pepper + Onion

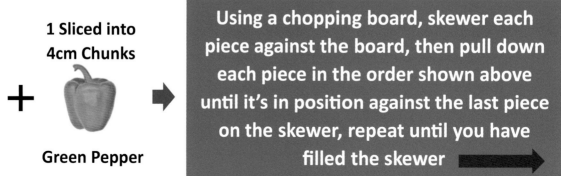

1 Sliced into 4cm Chunks → Using a chopping board, skewer each piece against the board, then pull down each piece in the order shown above until it's in position against the last piece on the skewer, repeat until you have filled the skewer ➡

Green Pepper

Brush or drizzle over the leftover marinade onto the prepared skewers	→	Grill for 15-20 minutes on a high heat turning 4-5 times

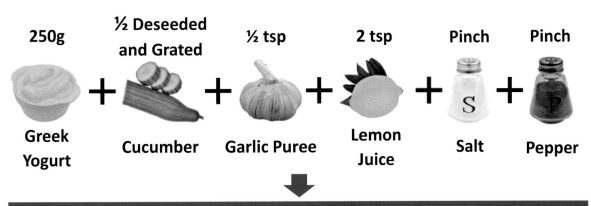

250g	½ Deseeded and Grated	½ tsp	2 tsp	Pinch	Pinch
Greek Yogurt	**Cucumber**	**Garlic Puree**	**Lemon Juice**	**Salt**	**Pepper**

With a paper towel, squeeze the excess water out of the grated cucumber, mix all the ingredients together and chill for at least 30 minutes

8 Large

→ Under the grill or in a toaster, heat through the pita bread for 1-2 minutes until lightly browned, slice along the long edge to open

Pita Bread

1 Sliced	4 Sliced	1 Sliced	160g Sliced
Little Gem Lettuce	**Tomatoes**	**Cucumber**	**Gherkins**

Bring together the kebabs, salad, pita bread and tzatziki

SERVE →

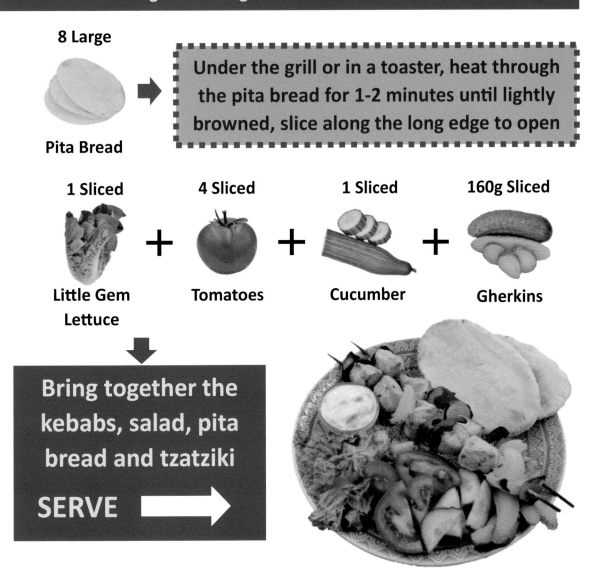

All Day Breakfast
Ingredients

1 Teaspoon Vegetable Oil

8 Pork Sausages

500 grams Potatoes

Water for Potatoes

2 Teaspoons Vegetable Oil

½ Teaspoon Salt

½ Teaspoon Black Pepper

1 Teaspoon Vegetable Oil

Knob of Butter

150 grams Button Mushrooms

Pinch of Black Pepper

2 Tomatoes

1 Teaspoon Vegetable Oil

240 grams Bacon (Back or Streaky)

1 Tin Beaked Beans (400 grams)

4 Tablespoons Olive Oil

4 Large Eggs (Free Range)

8 Slices of Bread

Butter for the Bread

NOTES;

The tomatoes can be cooked in the oven or on the hob for 5-10 minutes.

For vegan option replace all meat and dairy products for plant-based alternatives.

Always buy organic when possible.

All Day Breakfast

Love a good breakfast.   Set the oven to 220°c   Serves 4

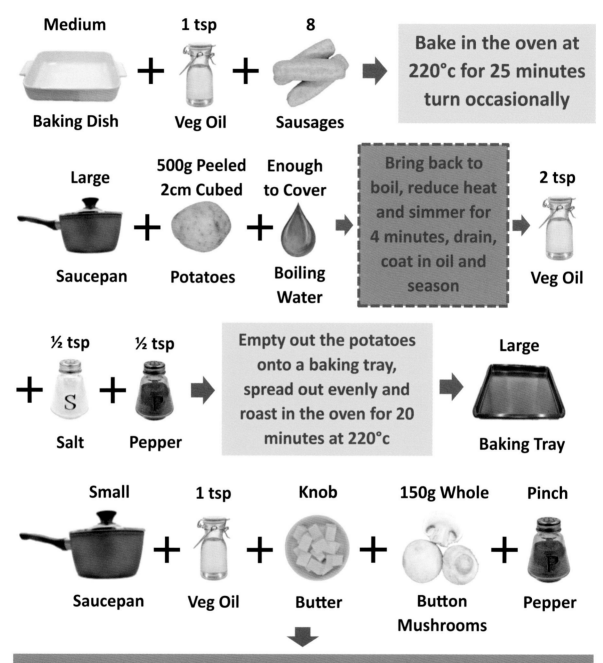

Medium
Baking Dish
+
1 tsp
Veg Oil
+
8
Sausages
➡
Bake in the oven at 220°c for 25 minutes turn occasionally

Large
Saucepan
+
500g Peeled 2cm Cubed
Potatoes
+
Enough to Cover
Boiling Water
➡
Bring back to boil, reduce heat and simmer for 4 minutes, drain, coat in oil and season
➡
2 tsp
Veg Oil

+
½ tsp
Salt
+
½ tsp
Pepper
➡
Empty out the potatoes onto a baking tray, spread out evenly and roast in the oven for 20 minutes at 220°c
➡
Large
Baking Tray

Small
Saucepan
+
1 tsp
Veg Oil
+
Knob
Butter
+
150g Whole
Button Mushrooms
+
Pinch
Pepper

Cook on a <u>lowest</u> heat for 10 minutes with the lid on. Holding the lid on, shake the saucepan often (instead of removing lid and stirring) <u>SET ASIDE</u> until serving. Whilst the sausages, potatoes and mushrooms are cooking, start the bacon, beans and eggs

➡

ADD 2 Halved Tomatoes → ADD TO THE TRAY WITH THE POTATOES OR SAUSAGES

Large
Frying Pan
+
1 tsp
Veg Oil
+
8 (240g)
Bacon
→
Fry bacon for 2-3 minutes each side on a med/high heat, wrap in foil and keep warm in the oven

Small
Saucepan
+
1 Tin (400g)
Baked Beans
→
Heat the beans gently for 5 minutes on a low heat stirring occasionally

Large
Frying Pan
+
4 Tbs
Olive Oil
+
4 Large
Eggs
→
Fry the eggs on a low heat for 5 minutes, use a large spoon to baste the eggs at the end of cooking time

8 Slices
Bread
+
Enough for 8 Slices
Butter
↓
Toast the bread to your liking and butter, bring everything together
SERVE →

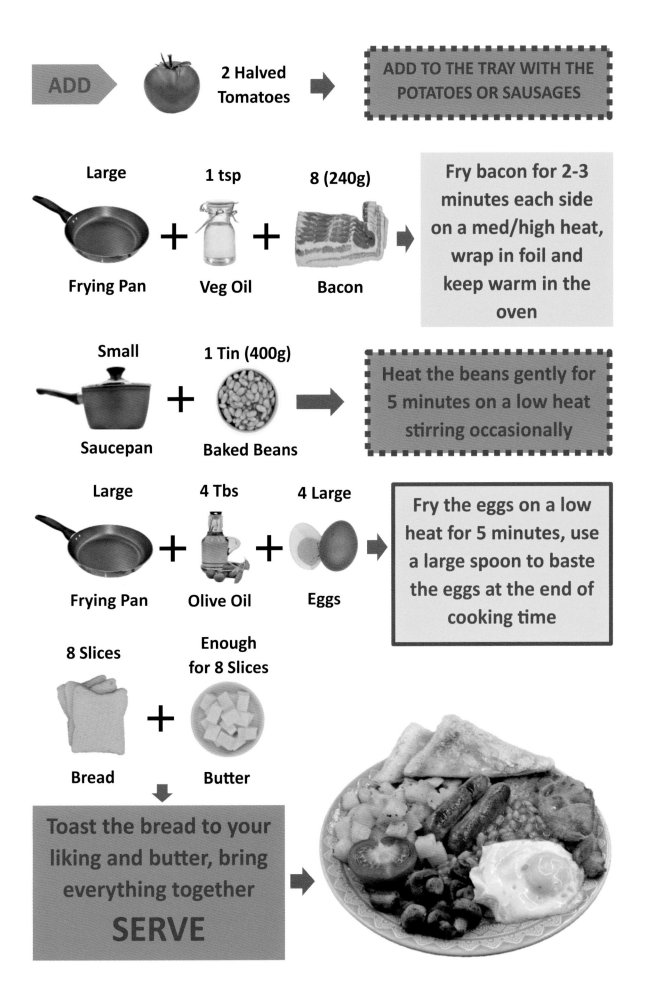

Mini Aubergine and fig Curry

Ingredients

2 Tablespoons Vegetable Oil

1 Large Onion

400 grams Mini Aubergines

4 Cloves Garlic

½ Teaspoon Salt

1 Tablespoon Mild Madras Curry Powder

500ml Water

1 Red Pepper

4 Green Chillies

1 Tablespoon Sugar

½ Teaspoon Black Pepper

2 Teaspoons Garam Masala

100 grams Partially Re-Hydrated Figs

700ml Water for Rice

350 grams Basmati Rice

75ml Boiling water

25 grams Wet Tamarind

2 Tablespoons Water

1 Tablespoon Corn Flour

30 grams Fresh Coriander

NOTES;

Use wet tamarind; it's sold in a block. Break off a piece about the volume of two stock cubes (25g), soak in hot water (75ml) for 5 minutes. Use a spoon to break it up then strain off the fibre (retaining the water). Alternatively, buy a tamarind paste.

Mini Aubergine and Fig Curry

Love curry, this one's delicious, sweet and spicey.

Serves 6

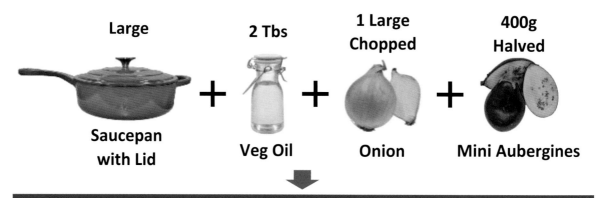

Large | 2 Tbs | 1 Large Chopped | 400g Halved

Saucepan with Lid + **Veg Oil** + **Onion** + **Mini Aubergines**

Fry on med/high heat for 3 minutes with lid on, shake pan often

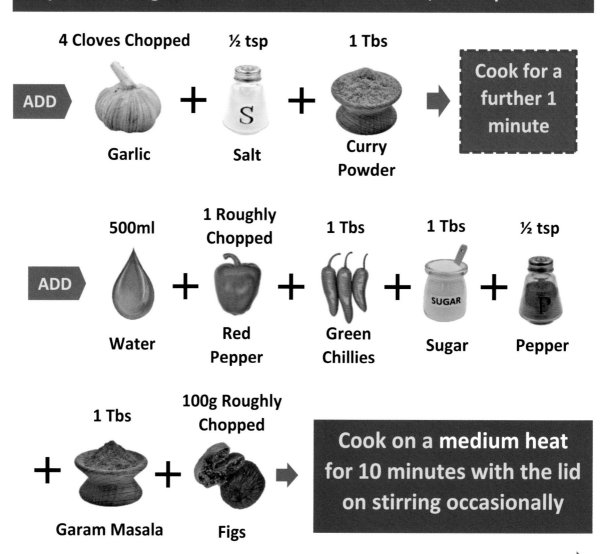

ADD 4 Cloves Chopped **Garlic** + ½ tsp **Salt** + 1 Tbs **Curry Powder** → **Cook for a further 1 minute**

ADD 500ml **Water** + 1 Roughly Chopped **Red Pepper** + 1 Tbs **Green Chillies** + 1 Tbs **Sugar** + ½ tsp **Pepper**

1 Tbs **Garam Masala** + 100g Roughly Chopped **Figs** → **Cook on a medium heat for 10 minutes with the lid on stirring occasionally**

Whilst the curry sauce is cooking start the rice	→	**Small** 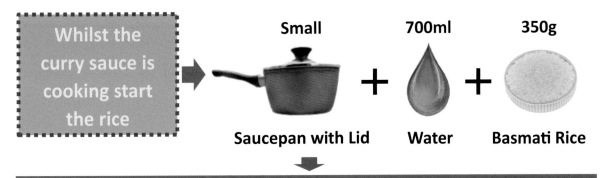 Saucepan with Lid	**+** **700ml** Water	**+** **350g** Basmati Rice

Cover and bring to the boil, then reduce to lowest heat for 5 minutes. Then, remove from heat and allow to rest for at least 10 minutes <u>SET ASIDE</u> until serving, <u>do not remove lid</u>

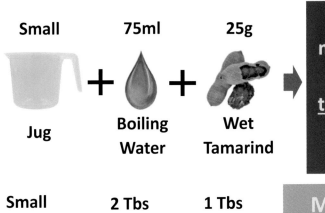

Small Jug **+** **75ml** Boiling Water **+** **25g** Wet Tamarind → Mix together, soak for 5 minutes then mash, sieve to remove seeds and <u>add the tamarind water to the curry</u>, the curry would have now cooked for 10 minutes

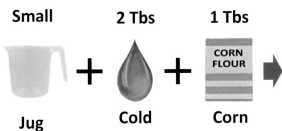

Small Jug **+** **2 Tbs** Cold Water **+** **1 Tbs** CORN FLOUR Corn Flour → Mix together and <u>add to the curry</u>, cook for a further 10 minutes on a medium heat, stirring occasionally

ADD TO THE CURRY

30g Chopped

Fresh Coriander

SERVE ▶

56

Meatloaf and Baked Beans
Ingredients

6 Tablespoons Tomato Ketchup

2 Tablespoons Cider Vinegar

2 Tablespoons Sugar

500g Minced Beef

1 Large Onion

2 Cloves Garlic

4 Tablespoons Tomato Ketchup

1 Teaspoon Worcester Sauce

75 grams Breadcrumbs

2 Stock Cubes

1 Teaspoon Mixed Herbs

2 Small Eggs

½ Teaspoon Salt

½ Teaspoon Black Pepper

Knob of Butter

1 Small Onion

2 Tins (800 grams) Haricot Beans

500 grams Passata

1 Tablespoon Tomato Puree

300ml Vegetable Stock

2 Tablespoons Sugar

Pinch of Cinnamon

1 Teaspoon Malt Vinegar

2 Tablespoons Olive Oil

2 Teaspoons Oregano

½ Teaspoon Salt

¼ Teaspoon Black Pepper

Water for Potatoes

1.2kg Potatoes

1 Teaspoon Salt

50ml Whole Milk

Knob of Butter

¼ Teaspoon Black Pepper

NOTES;

Serve with peas and gravy as an alternative for beans.

Use stock cubes that easily crumble, alternatively mix a stock cube with a small amount of boiling water to make a thin paste.

Meatloaf and Baked Beans

Looks great, tastes great, delicious!

Set oven to 180°c   Serves 6

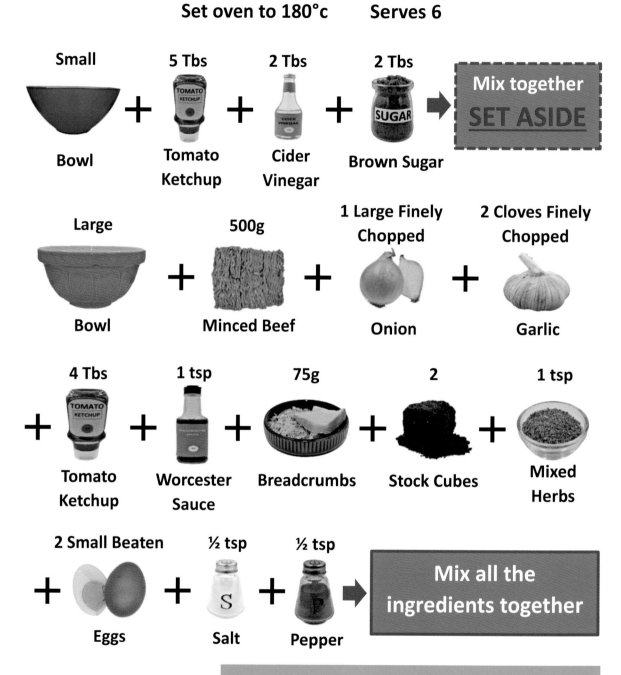

Small — Bowl
+
5 Tbs — Tomato Ketchup
+
2 Tbs — Cider Vinegar
+
2 Tbs — Brown Sugar
→ Mix together **SET ASIDE**

Large — Bowl
+
500g — Minced Beef
+
1 Large Finely Chopped — Onion
+
2 Cloves Finely Chopped — Garlic

+
4 Tbs — Tomato Ketchup
+
1 tsp — Worcester Sauce
+
75g — Breadcrumbs
+
2 — Stock Cubes
+
1 tsp — Mixed Herbs

+
2 Small Beaten — Eggs
+
½ tsp — Salt
+
½ tsp — Pepper
→ Mix all the ingredients together

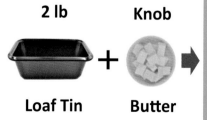

2 lb — Loaf Tin
+
Knob — Butter
→ Grease the tin with butter and fill with the meat mixture, firming down and smoothing the top, bake in the oven at **180°c** for 30 minutes, remove from oven, coat with the **SET-ASIDE** tomato sauce and bake for a further 30 minutes. Allow to rest for 10 minutes

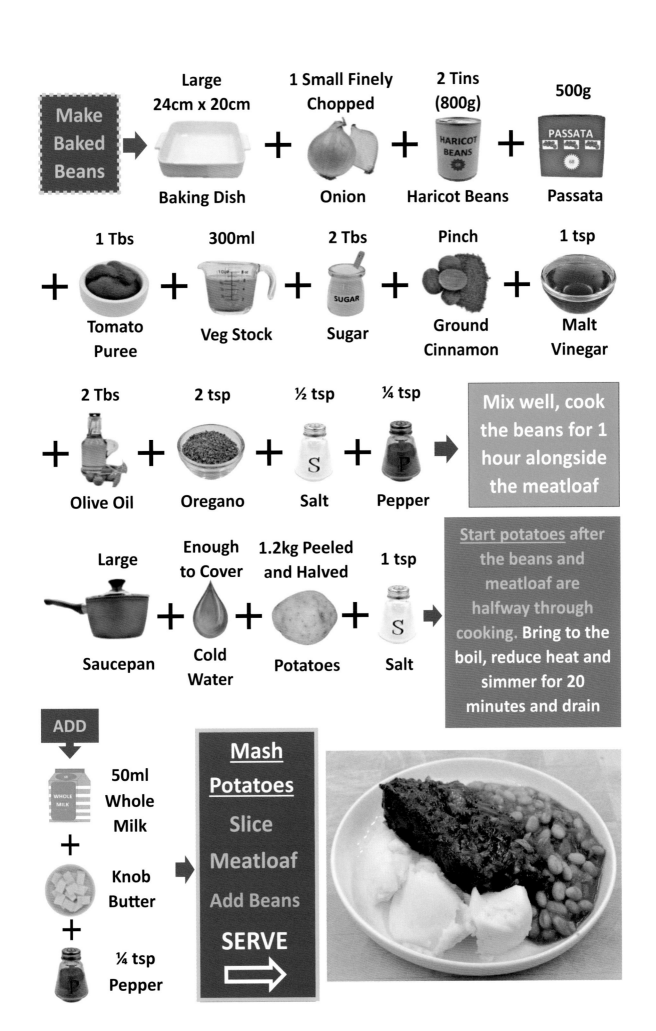

Make Baked Beans →

Large 24cm x 20cm — **Baking Dish**
+
1 Small Finely Chopped — **Onion**
+
2 Tins (800g) — **Haricot Beans**
+
500g — **Passata**

+
1 Tbs — **Tomato Puree**
+
300ml — **Veg Stock**
+
2 Tbs — **Sugar**
+
Pinch — **Ground Cinnamon**
+
1 tsp — **Malt Vinegar**

+
2 Tbs — **Olive Oil**
+
2 tsp — **Oregano**
+
½ tsp — **Salt**
+
¼ tsp — **Pepper**
→ Mix well, cook the beans for 1 hour alongside the meatloaf

Large — **Saucepan**
+
Enough to Cover — **Cold Water**
+
1.2kg Peeled and Halved — **Potatoes**
+
1 tsp — **Salt**
→ Start potatoes after the beans and meatloaf are halfway through cooking. Bring to the boil, reduce heat and simmer for 20 minutes and drain

ADD →
50ml Whole Milk
+
Knob Butter
+
¼ tsp Pepper

→ **Mash Potatoes** Slice Meatloaf Add Beans **SERVE** →

57

Beef Stroganoff
Ingredients

600 grams Cubed Beef

1 Tablespoon Plain Flour

1 Teaspoon Salt

1 Teaspoon Black Pepper

1 Tablespoon Olive Oil

2 Tablespoons Olive Oil

1 Large Onion

2 Cloves Garlic

1 Tablespoon Worcester Sauce

1 Tin (400ml) Mushroom Soup

300ml Beef Stock

Water for Potatoes

1.1kg Potatoes

1 Teaspoon Salt

50ml Whole Milk

50 grams Butter

¼ Teaspoon White Pepper

Water for Cabbage

1 Small Head of Spring Cabbage

NOTES;

For vegan option add an extra onion, replace dairy with plant-based, replace to vegetable stock, replace meat with large whole mushrooms and pulses. Mix 3 tablespoons of cornflour to 400ml water to replace the soup.

If not using tinned soup add 250g of sliced mushrooms and cook with the onion and garlic, add 400ml whole milk and 3 tablespoons corn flour.

Beef Stroganoff

Really easy, you can serve with rice.

Serves 6   Set oven to 190°c

600g Cubed — Beef
+ 1 Tbs — Plain Flour
+ 1 tsp — Salt (S)
+ 1 tsp — Pepper (P)
→ **COAT THE BEEF IN THE FLOUR AND SEASONING**

Large — Casserole Pot
+ 1 Tbs — Olive Oil
+ Seasoned — Beef
→ Fry beef for 5 minutes on a high heat, stir regularly to brown, remove the beef from the pot, SET ASIDE

Using the same pot ADD
→ 2 Tbs — Olive Oil
+ 1 Large Chopped — Onion
+ 2 Cloves Chopped — Garlic
+ 1 Tbs — Worcester Sauce

Fry for 5 minutes on a low heat, stirring regularly

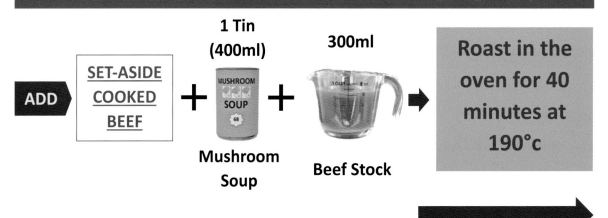

ADD → SET-ASIDE COOKED BEEF
+ 1 Tin (400ml) — Mushroom Soup
+ 300ml — Beef Stock
→ Roast in the oven for 40 minutes at 190°c

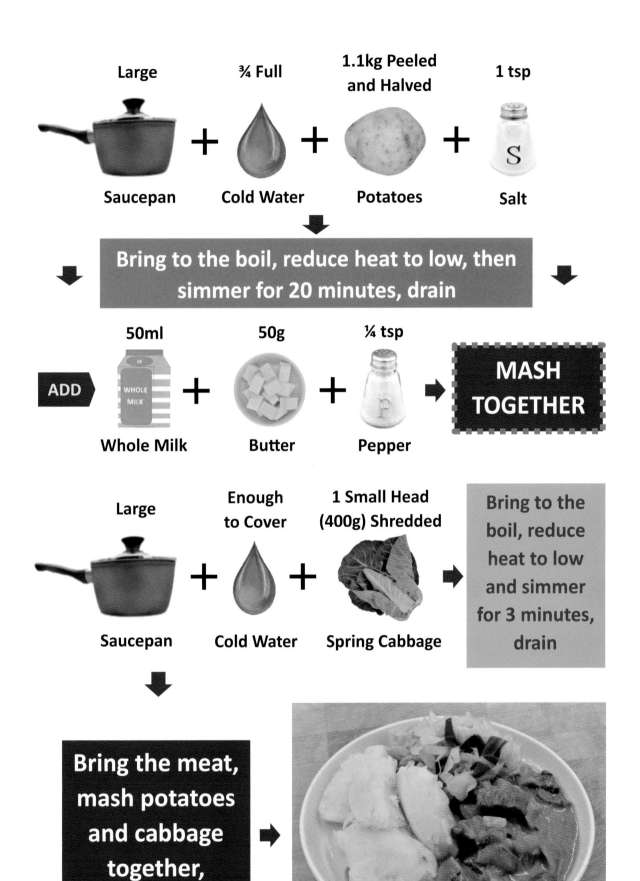

Large **Saucepan** + ¾ Full **Cold Water** + 1.1kg Peeled and Halved **Potatoes** + 1 tsp **Salt**

Bring to the boil, reduce heat to low, then simmer for 20 minutes, drain

ADD 50ml **Whole Milk** + 50g **Butter** + ¼ tsp **Pepper** → **MASH TOGETHER**

Large **Saucepan** + Enough to Cover **Cold Water** + 1 Small Head (400g) Shredded **Spring Cabbage** → **Bring to the boil, reduce heat to low and simmer for 3 minutes, drain**

Bring the meat, mash potatoes and cabbage together, SERVE

Salmon, Roast Veg and Salad

Ingredients

2 Tablespoon Olive Oil

2 (400 grams) Potatoes

2 (400 grams) Courgettes

1 Medium (400 grams) Sweet Potato

2 Large (400 grams) Carrots

3 Small Onions

1 Red Pepper

160 grams French Beans

6 Cloves Garlic

2 Teaspoons Mixed Herbs

½ Teaspoon Salt

1 Teaspoon Black Pepper

250 grams Cherry Tomatoes

4 Salmon Fillets (500 grams)

4 Slices of Lemon (1/2 Lemon)

4 Bay Leaves

Pinch of Salt and Pepper x 4

2 Sticks Celery

2 Apples (Gala)

50 grams Walnuts (Shelled)

100 grams Red Grapes

75 grams Mayonnaise

1 Tablespoon of Honey

1 Teaspoon Lemon Juice

Pinch of Salt

NOTES;

For vegan option, lightly fry slices of tofu, season with salt and pepper (replacing the fish). Use a plant-based mayonnaise and omit the honey.

Try toasting the walnuts in dry frying pan for 1 minute on a high heat before making the salad.

Salmon, Roast veg and Salad

The Waldorf salad compliments the fish and vegetables well.   Serves 4

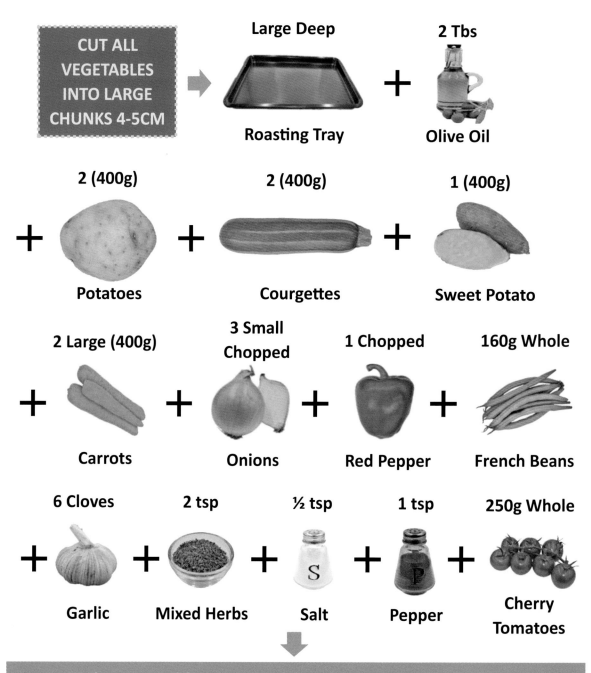

CUT ALL VEGETABLES INTO LARGE CHUNKS 4-5CM

Large Deep

Roasting Tray

2 Tbs

Olive Oil

2 (400g)

Potatoes

2 (400g)

Courgettes

1 (400g)

Sweet Potato

2 Large (400g)

Carrots

3 Small Chopped

Onions

1 Chopped

Red Pepper

160g Whole

French Beans

6 Cloves

Garlic

2 tsp

Mixed Herbs

½ tsp

Salt

1 tsp

Pepper

250g Whole

Cherry Tomatoes

Coat the vegetables in oil, add the seasonings and mix well, spread out evenly and add cherry tomatoes then roast in the oven at 200°c for 45 minutes. Turn half way through

2 x 40cm Lengths + **4 Fillets** + **4 Slices** + **4** + **Pinch**

Aluminium Foil + Salmon + Lemon + Bay Leaves + Salt and Pepper

Place two fillets in the middle of each piece of foil, lay a piece of lemon and a bay leaf on top of each fillet and season. Make parcels by bringing up the sides and crimping the edges together all along where the foil meets to resemble a kind of pasty shape. Place in the oven 12 minutes before the vegetables are due to finish cooking.

Medium + **2 Sticks Finely Chopped** + **2 Cored and Chopped** + **50g Roughly Chopped**

Bowl + Celery + Apples + Walnuts

100g Halved + **75g** + **1 Tbs** + **1 tsp** + **Pinch**

Grapes + Mayonnaise + Honey + Lemon + Salt

WHISK TOGETHER THE MAYONNAISE, HONEY, LEMON AND SALT BEFORE MIXING WITH THE REST OF THE INGREDIENTS OF THE WALDORF SALAD. BRING TOGETHER THE ROAST VEGETABLES, SALMON AND SALAD.

SERVE

59

Chinese Style Pork Chop
Ingredients

2 Teaspoons Vegetable Oil

750 grams Pork Chops

350 grams Carrots

250 grams Swede

150 grams Chestnut Mushrooms

25 grams Fresh Ginger

100 grams (1 Bunch) Spring Onions

200ml Vegetable Stock

800ml Water

2 Teaspoons Fish Sauce

2 Tablespoons Rice Wine

3 Tablespoons Light Soy Sauce

1 Teaspoon Dark Soy Sauce

2 Tablespoons Sugar

¼ Teaspoon White Pepper

3 Tablespoons Corn Flour

4 Tablespoons Water

30 grams Parsley

Water for Potatoes

1kg Potatoes

1 Teaspoon Salt

50ml Whole Milk

Knob of Butter

1 Small Egg

Pinch of Ground Pepper

NOTES;

For vegan option, omit the fish sauce, cook the stock and vegetables for 40 minutes, add 500 grams chestnut mushrooms, cook for the remaining 10 minutes.

You can omit the corn flour.

Any type of rice wine is fine to use.

Serve with noodles if you prefer.

Chinese Style Pork Chop

Really easy with little effort.

Serves 6

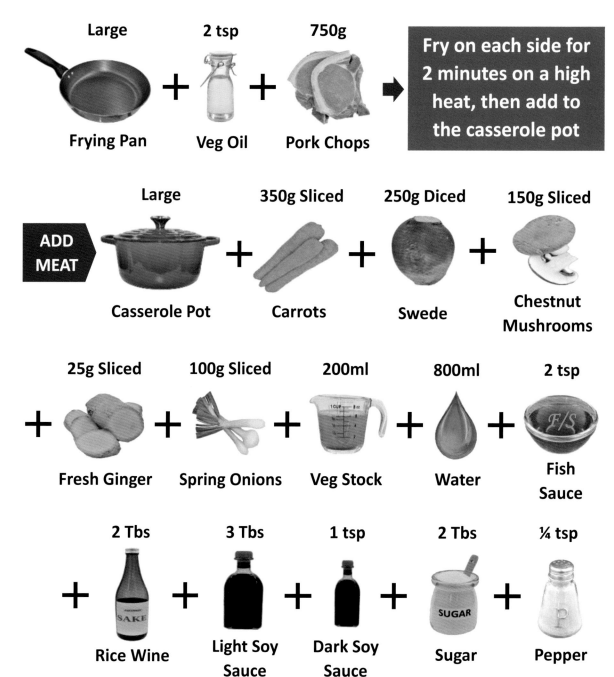

| Large | | 2 tsp | | 750g | | |
| Frying Pan | + | Veg Oil | + | Pork Chops | → | Fry on each side for 2 minutes on a high heat, then add to the casserole pot |

ADD MEAT →

| Large | | 350g Sliced | | 250g Diced | | 150g Sliced |
| Casserole Pot | + | Carrots | + | Swede | + | Chestnut Mushrooms |

| 25g Sliced | | 100g Sliced | | 200ml | | 800ml | | 2 tsp |
| Fresh Ginger | + | Spring Onions | + | Veg Stock | + | Water | + | Fish Sauce |

| 2 Tbs | | 3 Tbs | | 1 tsp | | 2 Tbs | | ¼ tsp |
| Rice Wine | + | Light Soy Sauce | + | Dark Soy Sauce | + | Sugar | + | Pepper |

Bring to boiling point, reduce heat to the lowest setting for 50 minutes →

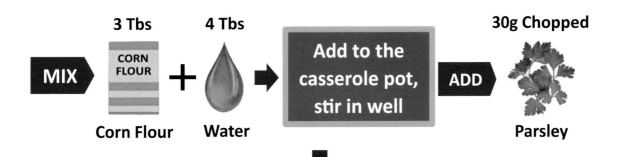

MIX 3 Tbs CORN FLOUR Corn Flour + 4 Tbs Water → Add to the casserole pot, stir in well **ADD** 30g Chopped Parsley

Stir in the parsley, your pork dish is ready to serve
While the pork is cooking start the mash

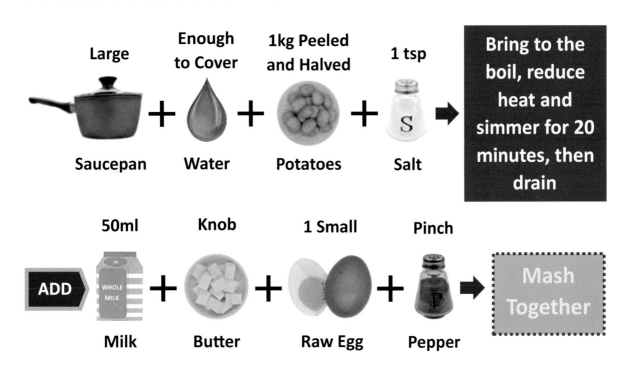

Large Saucepan + Enough to Cover Water + 1kg Peeled and Halved Potatoes + 1 tsp Salt → Bring to the boil, reduce heat and simmer for 20 minutes, then drain

ADD 50ml Milk + Knob Butter + 1 Small Raw Egg + Pinch Pepper → Mash Together

PLACE A SERVING OF MASH ON A PLATE, LAY OVER A PORK CHOP AND LADLE OVER THE GRAVY

SERVE →

Chicken Nuggets
Ingredients

2 Tablespoons Olive Oil

1.2kg Large Potatoes

½ tsp Sweet Paprika

2 tsp Garlic Granules

½ Teaspoon Salt

¼ Teaspoon Black Pepper

2 Tablespoons Olive Oil

750ml Chicken Breast

½ Teaspoon Salt

½ Teaspoon Black Pepper

4 Tablespoon Flour

2 Small Eggs

100 grams Panko Breadcrumbs

5 Cobs Sweetcorn

Water for Sweetcorn

½ Teaspoon Salt

50 grams Butter

NOTES;

Try different sets of seasoning for your potato wedges.

Delicious served with sour cream, salsa and other dips.

For a vegan alternative, break up a head of cauliflower, coat in the seasoned oil adding some chopped chillies and a teaspoon of cumin seeds and bake in the same way.

Chicken Nuggets

Really easy and really tasty, equally good with mash and baked beans.　　**Serves 5**

Large	2 Tbs	1.2kg Cut in Wedges	½ tsp	2 tsp
Baking Tray	Olive Oil	Potatoes	Paprika	Garlic Granules

½ tsp	¼ tsp	
Salt	Pepper	Mix together (on the baking tray) and bake in the oven for 35 minutes, turn halfway through cooking

Large	2 Tbs	750g Sliced 3cm Slices	½ tsp	½ tsp
Bowl	Olive Oil	Chicken Breast	Salt	Pepper

Mix together, shake off the excess oil. On a plate dust the chicken pieces with flour **SET ASIDE**

Large	4 Tbs
Plate	Flour

Medium

Bowl

+

2 Small

Eggs

→

Beat the eggs together. A piece at a time, coat the chicken pieces in egg, then in the breadcrumb

→

100g

Breadcrumbs

→ Spread the breaded chicken pieces out on a baking tray, and bake in the oven (15-20 minutes) alongside the wedges, turning halfway through cooking

Large

Baking Tray

Large

Saucepan

+

5 Cobs

Sweetcorn

+

Enough to Cover

Boiling Water

+

½ tsp

S

Salt

→

Bring back to the boil, then reduce heat to low and simmer for 3 minutes, drain

50g Cubed

Butter

+

Cooked

Sweetcorn

→

Put the butter into the hot saucepan and coat the cobs of corn in the melted butter

Bring the wedges, chicken nuggets and corn together
SERVE

→

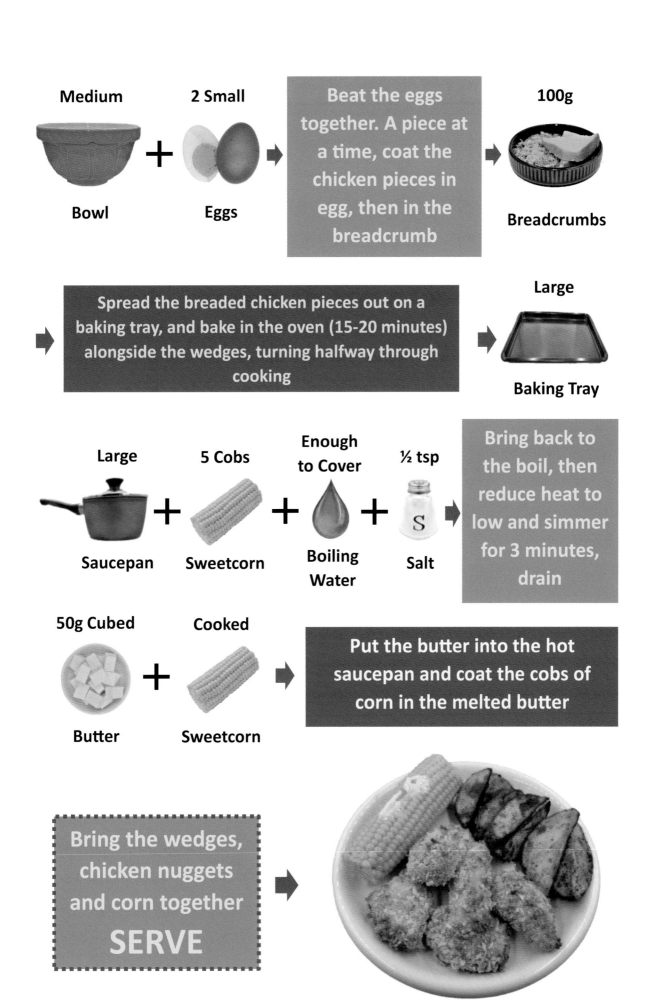

61

Curried Fish

Ingredients

600ml Cold Water

300 grams Basmati Rice

2 Tablespoons Vegetable Oil

2 Small Shallots (80 grams)

2 Cloves Garlic

2cm Cube Fresh Ginger

8cm Stick of Cinnamon

2 Whole Cardamom

1 Teaspoon Cumin Seeds

1 Teaspoon Fennel Seeds

8 Whole Fresh Curry Leaves

3 Whole Chillies

1 Tablespoon Tomato Puree

2 Tablespoons Water

6 Large Tomatoes

350ml Chicken Stock

1 Tablespoon Lemon Juice

½ Teaspoon Salt

600 grams Cod Fillets

1 Tablespoon Turmeric

¼ Teaspoon Black Pepper

4 Tablespoons Vegetable Oil

1 Teaspoon Garam Masala

1 Teaspoon Asafoetida

15 grams Fresh Coriander

NOTES;

For vegan option replace fish with carrot batons and sweet potato batons, use a vegetable stock or water.

Take care when lifting the fish into the curry.

Use any type of white fish.

Curried Fish

Any white fish could be used with this curry. Try different spices, create a new curry.   Serves 4

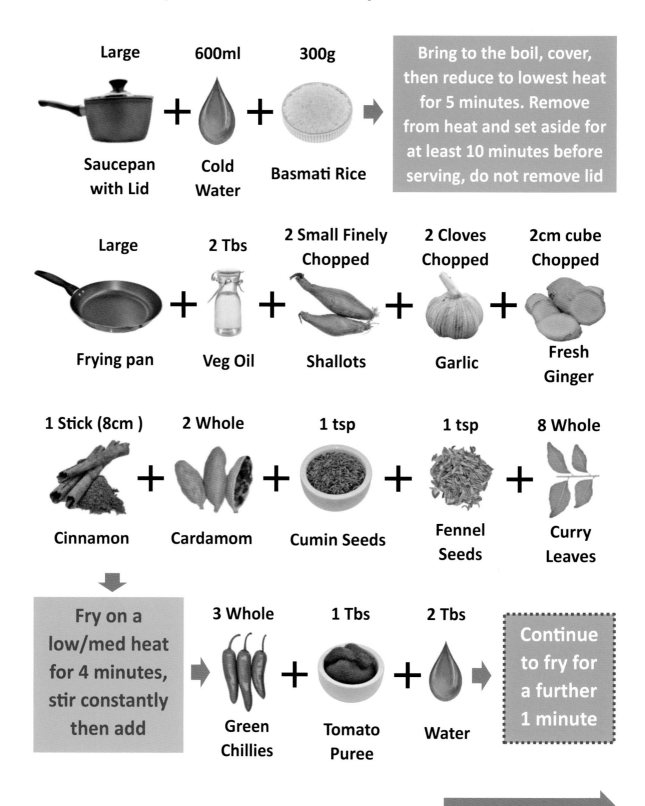

Large — Saucepan with Lid

+

600ml — Cold Water

+

300g — Basmati Rice

→ Bring to the boil, cover, then reduce to lowest heat for 5 minutes. Remove from heat and set aside for at least 10 minutes before serving, do not remove lid

Large — Frying pan

+

2 Tbs — Veg Oil

+

2 Small Finely Chopped — Shallots

+

2 Cloves Chopped — Garlic

+

2cm cube Chopped — Fresh Ginger

1 Stick (8cm) — Cinnamon

+

2 Whole — Cardamom

+

1 tsp — Cumin Seeds

+

1 tsp — Fennel Seeds

+

8 Whole — Curry Leaves

Fry on a low/med heat for 4 minutes, stir constantly then add

3 Whole — Green Chillies

+

1 Tbs — Tomato Puree

+

2 Tbs — Water

→ Continue to fry for a further 1 minute

ADD

6 Large Chopped — Tomatoes **+** 350ml — Chicken Stock **+** 1 Tbs — Lemon Juice **+** 1 tsp — Palm Sugar **+** ½ tsp — Salt

Increase heat to high, cook on a medium heat for 15 minutes, stirring regularly. While cooking, start the fish

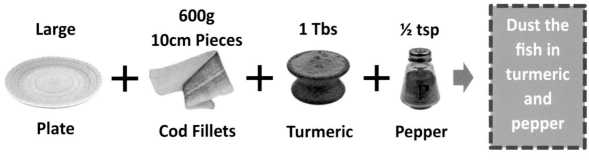

Large — Plate **+** 600g 10cm Pieces — Cod Fillets **+** 1 Tbs — Turmeric **+** ½ tsp — Pepper → Dust the fish in turmeric and pepper

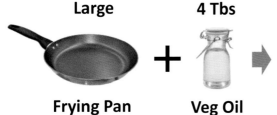

Large — Frying Pan **+** 4 Tbs — Veg Oil → Fry the fish on a med/high heat for 1 minute each side

ADD the fish to the tomato curry mixture **+** 1 tsp — Garam Masala **+** 1 tsp — Asafoetida → Cook for 10 minutes on a med/low heat

SPRINKLE OVER

15g Chopped

Fresh Coriander

SERVE WITH RICE

Sausage Casserole
Ingredients

2 Tablespoon Olive Oil

700 grams Pork Sausages (12)

1 Large Onion

120 grams Leeks

4 Cloves Garlic

2 Sticks of Celery

110 grams French Beans

100ml Red Wine

1 Tablespoon Light Brown Sugar

750ml Chicken Stock

1 Tin Chopped Tomatoes (400 grams)

300 grams Basmati Rice

1 Teaspoon Salt

½ Teaspoon Black Pepper

500ml Chicken Stock

2 Tins (800 grams) Plum Tomatoes

1 Tin (400 grams) Butter Beans

½ Teaspoon Sweet Paprika

½ Teaspoon Salt

½ Teaspoon Black Pepper

2 Whole Bay Leaves

1 Teaspoon Mixed Herbs

1 Tablespoon Lemon Juice

Water for Potatoes

1.2kg Potatoes

NOTES;

Wash the leeks well.

Serve with rice instead of potatoes.

For vegan option replace stock to vegetable, use plant-based sausages.

Sausage Casserole

A comfort food, great with potatoes or rice.

Set the oven to 200°c   Serves 6

| Large | | 2 Tbs | | 700g | |
| Casserole Pot | + | Olive Oil | + | Sausages | → Fry the sausages for 6 minutes on a med/low heat, turning frequently until nicely browned, remove from pot SET ASIDE |

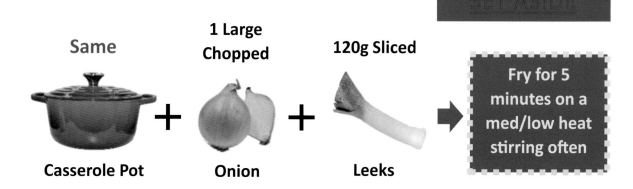

| Same | | 1 Large Chopped | | 120g Sliced | |
| Casserole Pot | + | Onion | + | Leeks | → Fry for 5 minutes on a med/low heat stirring often |

| ADD | 4 Cloves Chopped | | 2 Sticks | | 110g Halved | |
| | Garlic | + | Celery | + | French Beans | → Increase heat to high, continue cooking for another 2 minutes |

| ADD | 100ml | | 1 Tbs | | | | ADD | 500ml |
| | Red Wine | + | Brown Sugar | → Cook for 2-3 minutes, stirring gently | | | Chicken Stock |

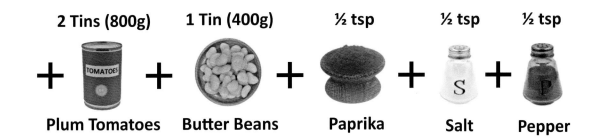

2 Tins (800g)	1 Tin (400g)	½ tsp	½ tsp	½ tsp
Plum Tomatoes	Butter Beans	Paprika	Salt	Pepper

2 Whole	1 tsp	1 Tbs	
Bay Leaves	Mixed Herbs	Lemon Juice	Cover and bake in the oven at 200°c for 15 minutes

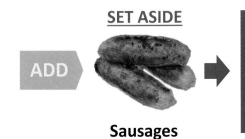

SET ASIDE

ADD — Sausages

Mix in the sausages and cook uncovered for a further 25 minutes **START POTATOES**

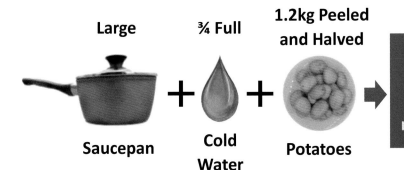

Large	¾ Full	1.2kg Peeled and Halved	
Saucepan	Cold Water	Potatoes	Bring to boiling point, reduce heat to low and simmer for 15-20 minutes, drain and serve

SERVE THE SAUSAGE CASSEROLE AND BOILED POTATOES TOGETHER

YOUR NOTES

Chicken Curry
Ingredients

2 Tablespoons Vegetable Oil

30 grams Butter

1 Large Onion

1 Apple (Gala)

2 Cloves Garlic

2cm Cube Fresh Ginger

2 Tablespoons Mild Curry Powder

10cm Cinnamon Stick

3 Whole Green Chillies

8 Fresh Curry Leaves

1 Tablespoons Tomato Puree

1 Tin Tomatoes (400 grams)

½ Teaspoon Salt

½ Teaspoon Black Pepper

1 Tablespoon Palm Sugar

600ml Chicken Stock

750 grams Chicken Breast

75 grams Sultanas

2 Tablespoons Mango Chutney

2 Tablespoons Corn Flour

3 Tablespoons Water

700ml Water for Rice

350 grams Basmati Rice

15 grams Fresh Coriander

NOTES;

For vegan option replace stock to vegetable, use vegan butter, use butternut squash instead of chicken or courgettes and aubergines.

Chicken Curry

A nice fruity curry, mild yet distinct.   Serves 6

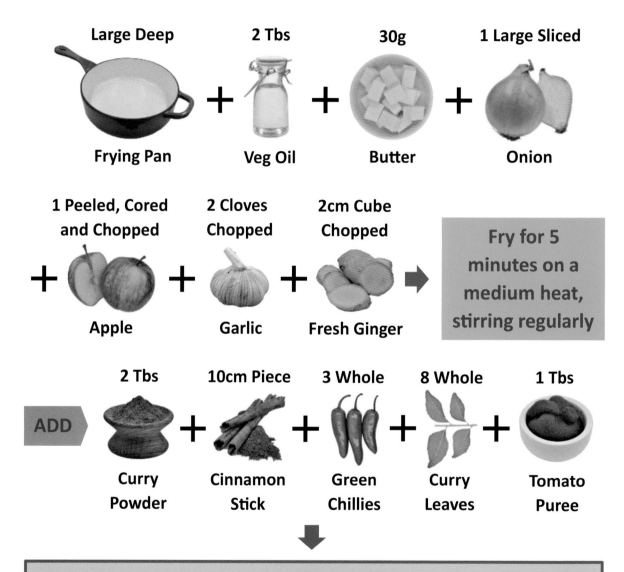

Large Deep — Frying Pan

2 Tbs — Veg Oil

30g — Butter

1 Large Sliced — Onion

1 Peeled, Cored and Chopped — Apple

2 Cloves Chopped — Garlic

2cm Cube Chopped — Fresh Ginger

Fry for 5 minutes on a medium heat, stirring regularly

ADD

2 Tbs — Curry Powder

10cm Piece — Cinnamon Stick

3 Whole — Green Chillies

8 Whole — Curry Leaves

1 Tbs — Tomato Puree

Continue cooking for a further 1 minute, stir continually

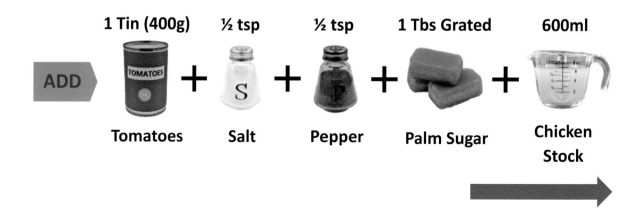

ADD

1 Tin (400g) — Tomatoes

½ tsp — Salt

½ tsp — Pepper

1 Tbs Grated — Palm Sugar

600ml — Chicken Stock

750g Cubed

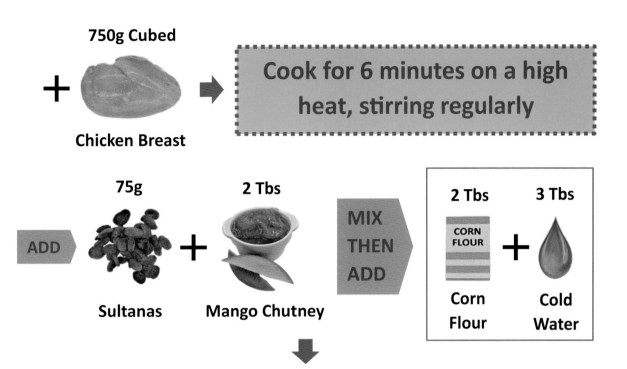

Chicken Breast

Cook for 6 minutes on a high heat, stirring regularly

ADD

75g Sultanas + **2 Tbs** Mango Chutney

MIX THEN ADD

2 Tbs Corn Flour + **3 Tbs** Cold Water

Cook uncovered for 20 minutes on a med/low heat stirring occasionally

Medium Saucepan with Lid + **700ml** Cold Water + **350g** Basmati Rice

Bring to the boil, cover, then reduce to lowest heat for 5 minutes. Then remove from heat and SET ASIDE for at least 10 minutes before serving, do not remove lid

15g Chopped Fresh Coriander

MIX INTO THE CURRY CORIANDER, SERVE THE CURRY WITH THE RICE

Spaghetti Carbonara

Ingredients

Water for Pasta

500 grams Spaghetti

1 Teaspoon Olive Oil

25 grams Butter

1 Small Onion

2 Cloves Garlic

½ Teaspoon Black Pepper

240 grams Bacon

150ml Single Cream

3 Small Eggs

150 grams Medium Cheddar

Pinch Salt

15 grams Fresh Parsley

NOTES;

For vegan option, replace the dairy with vegan alternatives, use soya bacon strips or vegan ham.

Another vegan alternative is to make a white sauce and add vegan bacon or ham (white sauce recipe can be found on recipe 14, which can be easily tailored to your taste).

Cooked ham can be used, don't cook it for 5 minutes like the bacon but perhaps just a minute.

The heat within the pasta, cooks the egg.

Spaghetti Carbonara

A classic dish, really easy and really tasty.

Serves 6

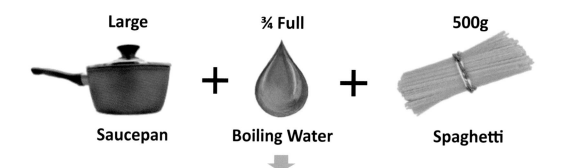

Large	¾ Full	500g
Saucepan	Boiling Water	Spaghetti

Bring back to the boil, stir with fork, reduce heat to low and simmer for 9-10 minutes, drain then <u>SET ASIDE</u>

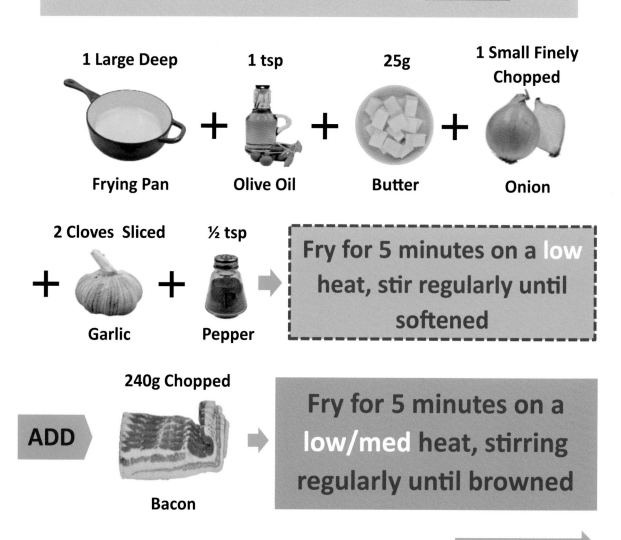

1 Large Deep	1 tsp	25g	1 Small Finely Chopped
Frying Pan	Olive Oil	Butter	Onion

2 Cloves Sliced	½ tsp
Garlic	Pepper

Fry for 5 minutes on a low heat, stir regularly until softened

ADD — 240g Chopped Bacon

Fry for 5 minutes on a low/med heat, stirring regularly until browned

While the bacon is cooking mix the cream and eggs together

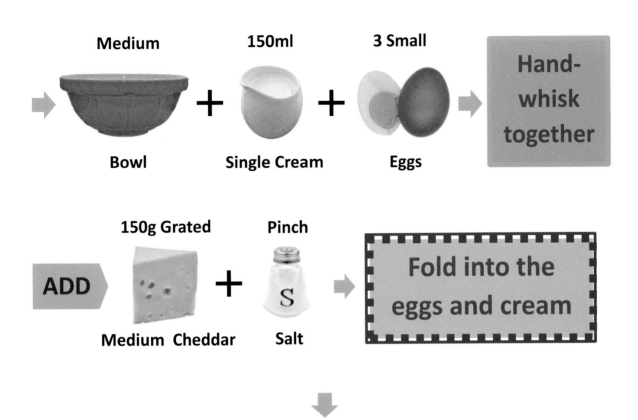

Medium
Bowl
+
150ml
Single Cream
+
3 Small
Eggs
Hand-whisk together

ADD
150g Grated
Medium Cheddar
+
Pinch
Salt
Fold into the eggs and cream

Mix the SET-ASIDE pasta into the bacon mixture, remove from heat and mix in well the cream and egg mixture and the parsley

MIX IN
15g Chopped
Fresh Parsley
SERVE

Ratatouille

Ingredients

2 Tablespoon Olive Oil

1 Large Onion

2 Cloves Garlic

½ Teaspoon Black Pepper

1 Large Courgette (300 grams)

1 Medium Aubergine (300 grams)

1 Red Pepper

1 Green Pepper

Juice of Half a Lemon

1 Tablespoon Oregano

400ml Water

200ml Vegetable Stock

1 Teaspoon Salt

10 grams Fresh Basil

1 Tablespoon Sugar

3 Large Tomatoes

Water for Potatoes

1.2kg Potatoes

1 Teaspoon Salt

50ml Whole Milk

1 Small Egg

Knob of Butter

50 grams Spring Onions

Water for Asparagus

200 grams Asparagus

NOTES;

For vegan option, use plant-based dairy alternatives.

Can be blended into a pasta sauce or a base for another creation, like a vegetable pasta bake.

Ratatouille

Really versatile dish, can be blended into a lovely
pasta sauce.   Set oven to 200°c   Serves 6

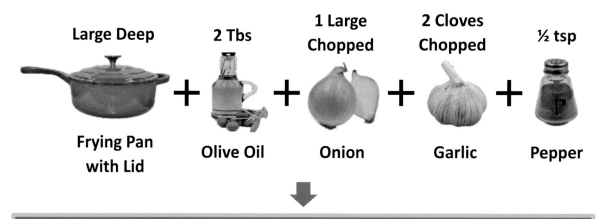

Large Deep — Frying Pan with Lid

+

2 Tbs — Olive Oil

+

1 Large Chopped — Onion

+

2 Cloves Chopped — Garlic

+

½ tsp — Pepper

Fry for 5 minutes on a med/low heat, stirring regularly

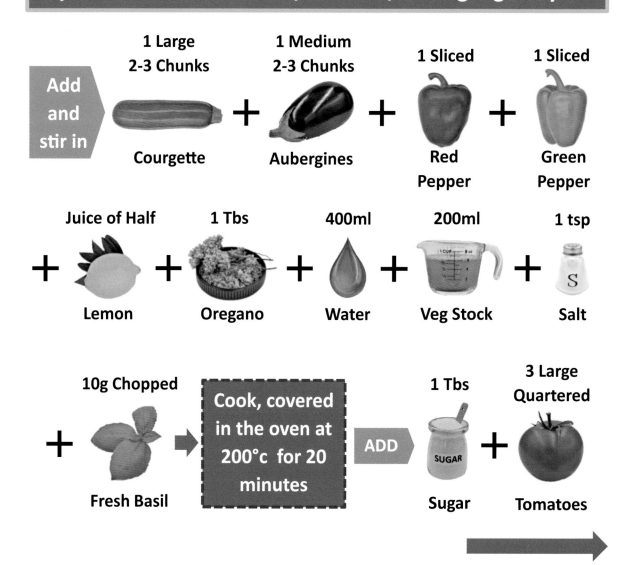

Add and stir in

1 Large 2-3 Chunks — Courgette

+

1 Medium 2-3 Chunks — Aubergines

+

1 Sliced — Red Pepper

+

1 Sliced — Green Pepper

+

Juice of Half — Lemon

+

1 Tbs — Oregano

+

400ml — Water

+

200ml — Veg Stock

+

1 tsp — Salt

+

10g Chopped — Fresh Basil

Cook, covered in the oven at 200°c for 20 minutes

ADD

1 Tbs — Sugar

+

3 Large Quartered — Tomatoes

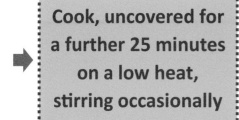

Cook, uncovered for a further 25 minutes on a low heat, stirring occasionally

Whilst the ratatouille's cooking start the potatoes and vegetables

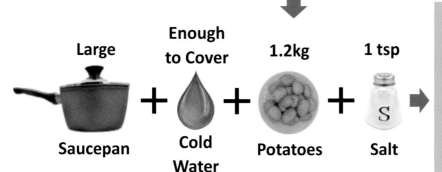

Large **Saucepan** + Enough to Cover **Cold Water** + 1.2kg **Potatoes** + 1 tsp **Salt**

Bring to the boil, then reduce heat to low, simmer for 15-20 minutes until cooked through, drain

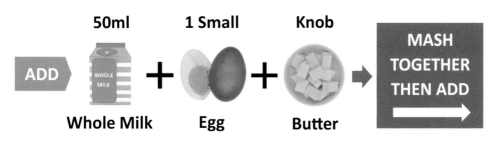

ADD 50ml **Whole Milk** + 1 Small **Egg** + Knob **Butter**

MASH TOGETHER THEN ADD →

50g Chopped **Spring Onions**

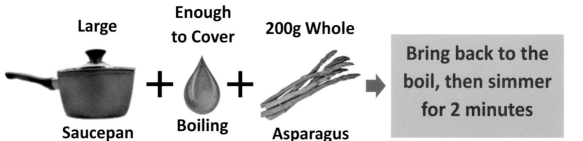

Large **Saucepan** + Enough to Cover **Boiling Water** + 200g Whole **Asparagus**

Bring back to the boil, then simmer for 2 minutes

BRING TOGETHER THE RATATOUILLE THE MASH POTATOES AND THE ASPARAGUS

SERVE

Vegetable Pie
Ingredients

200 grams Plain Flour

60 grams Butter

40 grams Lard

Pinch of Salt

60-80ml Chilled Water

2 Tablespoons Olive Oil

250 grams Swede

200 grams Carrots

150 grams Leeks

2 Cloves Garlic

1 Whole Bay Leaf

½ Teaspoon Black Pepper

400ml Vegetable Stock

1 Stick Celery

1 Small Head of Broccoli

½ Teaspoon Salt

3 Tablespoons Olive Oil

4 Tablespoons Plain Flour

250ml Whole Milk

1 Small Egg

NOTES;

When straining the vegetables place a sieve or colander over a large bowl and collect as much stock as possible.

For vegan option replace the butter and lard with a plant-based butter and the milk with soya milk, brush pastry with soya milk also.

Vegetable Pie

Many variations can be created. Also serve this pie with roast potatoes and peas.   Set oven to 200°c   Serves 5

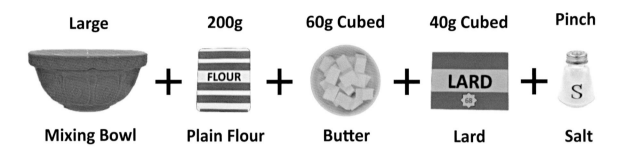

Large	200g	60g Cubed	40g Cubed	Pinch
Mixing Bowl	Plain Flour	Butter	Lard	Salt

Sift the flour into the bowl, and with your fingertips rub together until the mixture resembles breadcrumbs, add the water, <u>a little at a time</u> until a stiff but soft dough is formed. Wrap in cling film and refrigerate for half an hour. START THE FILLING

60-80ml

Water

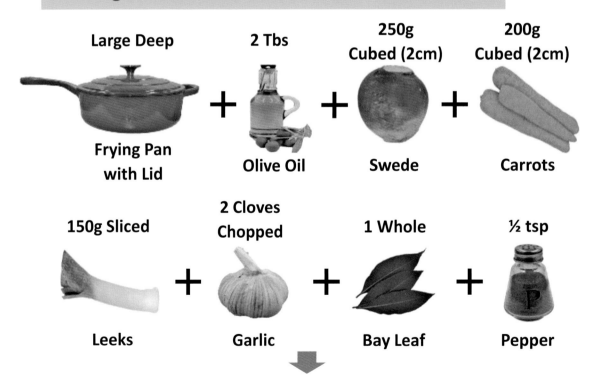

Large Deep	2 Tbs	250g Cubed (2cm)	200g Cubed (2cm)
Frying Pan with Lid	Olive Oil	Swede	Carrots

150g Sliced	2 Cloves Chopped	1 Whole	½ tsp
Leeks	Garlic	Bay Leaf	Pepper

Fry on a med/high heat stirring regularly for 10 minutes

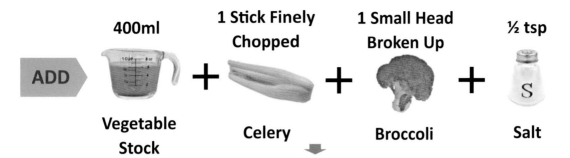

ADD

400ml	1 Stick Finely Chopped	1 Small Head Broken Up	½ tsp
Vegetable Stock	Celery	Broccoli	Salt

Bring to the boil, cover, then reduce heat to low and simmer for 6 minutes, drain reserving the liquid, remove the bay leaf   SET ALL ASIDE

Large	3 Tbs	4 Tbs	250ml	
Frying pan	Olive Oil	Plain Flour	Whole Milk	SET- ASIDE LIQUID

Cook the flour for 1 minute on a low heat, stirring continuously then add, slowly, the milk and reserved (SET ASIDE) liquid, bring to boiling point, until thickened and smooth, stir continuously

Large	SET-ASIDE VEGETABLE	WHITE SAUCE	Mix together the vegetables and sauce carefully and fill the pie dish
Pie Dish			

On a floured surface, roll out the pastry about 5mm thick and slightly larger than the pie dish you are using. Place on top of the dish, and with a knife cut off the excess pastry from around the dish. Use the excess pastry to decorate the pie with some leaf shapes. Brush with beaten egg and with a knife make 6-8 slits in the pastry for the steam to escape.
Bake for 35 minutes at 200°c

1 Small Egg Beaten

Bake in the middle of the oven at 200°c for 35 minutes

SERVE

YOUR NOTES

Ravioli Pinwheels
Ingredients

1 Tablespoon Olive Oil

1 Small Onion

2 Cloves Garlic

½ Teaspoon Black Pepper

1 Tablespoon Tomato Puree

3 Large Tomatoes

300 grams Cherry Tomatoes

1 Tablespoon Lemon Juice

2 Teaspoons Sugar

½ Teaspoon Salt

20 grams Fresh Basil

1 ½ Tablespoons Corn Flour

350ml Cold Water

375 grams Minced Beef

½ Teaspoon Salt

½ Teaspoon Black Pepper

2 Teaspoons Oregano

240g Plain Flour

2 Large Eggs

Pinch of Salt

1-3 Tablespoons Water

Water for Pasta

NOTES;

Good Tip; Use the meat in a sausage to fill the pasta.

When mixing the dough, the amount of water needed, varies because the egg size will vary.

Limitless variations can be made, even add seeds to the pasta dough.

When rolling out the dough use plenty of flour on the work surface.

For vegetarian option For the filling (in 75g portions) grate finely some butternut squash (45g) put it into a mortar and pestle along with some toasted pine nuts (3g) and butter beans (7g), season and pound into a semi-paste, mix in some ricotta cheese (20g) and build the pinwheel in the same way.

You can create many different fillings, keep to 75g per pasta ring.

Ravioli Pinwheels

During testing I created this technique for making a fresh ravioli pasta. It works well because of the spiral created, and when cooked, the pasta expands holding on to the filling. When cut, the pieces form a pinwheel. Also allows you to easily make fresh pasta without being an expert. Delicious!   SERVES 4

Large	1 Tbs	1 Small Chopped	2 Cloves Chopped	½ tsp
Frying Pan	Olive Oil	Onion	Garlic	Pepper

Fry for 4 minutes on a med/low heat, stir regularly until softened

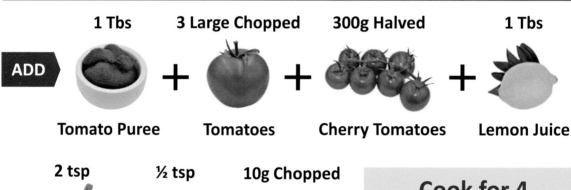

ADD

1 Tbs	3 Large Chopped	300g Halved	1 Tbs
Tomato Puree	Tomatoes	Cherry Tomatoes	Lemon Juice

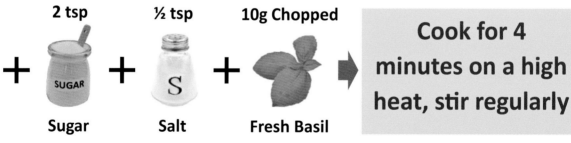

2 tsp	½ tsp	10g Chopped
Sugar	Salt	Fresh Basil

Cook for 4 minutes on a high heat, stir regularly

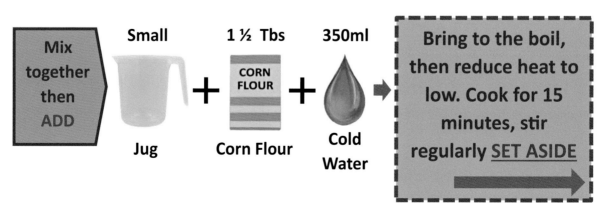

Mix together then ADD

Small	1 ½ Tbs	350ml
Jug	Corn Flour	Cold Water

Bring to the boil, then reduce heat to low. Cook for 15 minutes, stir regularly SET ASIDE

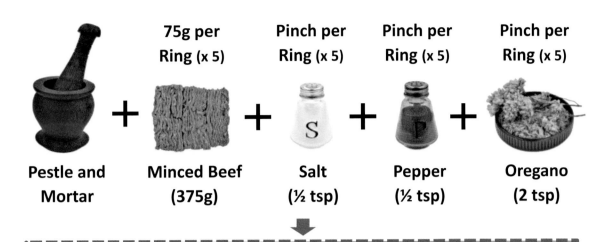

Pestle and Mortar	Minced Beef (375g)	Salt (½ tsp)	Pepper (½ tsp)	Oregano (2 tsp)
	75g per Ring (x 5)	Pinch per Ring (x 5)	Pinch per Ring (x 5)	Pinch per Ring (x 5)

Pound the beef and seasonings into a semi-paste (in 75g portions) SET ASIDE

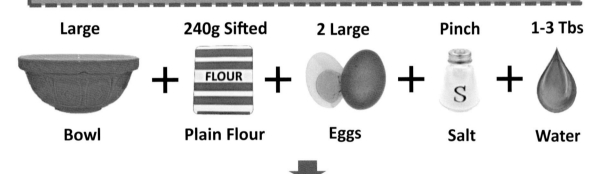

Bowl	Plain Flour	Eggs	Salt	Water
Large	240g Sifted	2 Large	Pinch	1-3 Tbs

Mix together well, forming a firm dough ball.

Flour the work surface well and take a piece of dough of about 75 grams

Roll out the dough to about 1-2mm thick and into a rectangle 30cm x 15cm

Spread out the <u>SET- ASIDE</u> filling, (75g) covering 2/3 of the pasta sheet

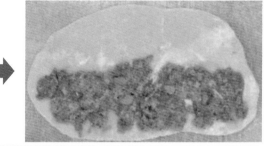

Roll up the pasta sheet starting at the long edge

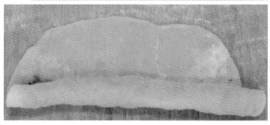

Wet the closing edge with water to seal, then join both ends by pinching firmly together

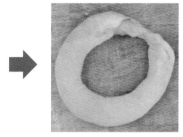

Large   ¾ Full   5 Rings

Saucepan   Boiling Water   Pasta Rings

Once made, keep rings separate on a floured surface. Drop in the water, individually

Bring back to the boil then reduce heat and simmer for 6 minutes. Use tongs to remove them from the water. On a chopping board, slice to form PINWHEELS

Cooked and sliced <u>Pinwheels</u>

Mix the sauce and the pinwheels together **SERVE**

Here's an idea...

As all the recipes have mini-recipes and methods for cooking, try mixing and matching.

For Example;

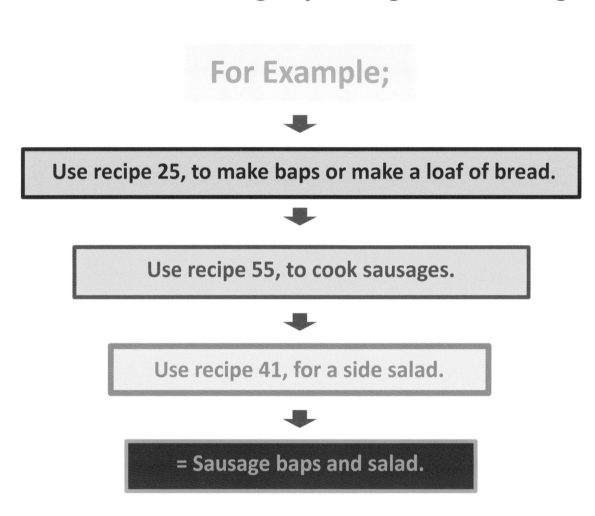

Use recipe 25, to make baps or make a loaf of bread.

Use recipe 55, to cook sausages.

Use recipe 41, for a side salad.

= Sausage baps and salad.

MORE BOOKS TO FOLLOW...

Creating this book was a challenge, a challenge for me and no doubt challenging for my family and friends.

So, I would like to thank my family for supporting me with their patience and my best friend Lara Jones for helping me in so many ways with ideas, cooking, research, marketing and for putting up with my idiosyncrasies, thank you Lara.

Also, I'd like to thank Spiffing Publishers for their technical support in helping to bring the book to the market.